The Small Group Book

The Practical Guide for Nurturing Christians and Building Churches

Dale Galloway
with Kathi Mills

Fleming H. Revell
A Division of Baker Book House Co
Grand Rapids, Michigan 49516

© 1995 by Dale Galloway and Kathi Mills

Published by Fleming H. Revell
a division of Baker Book House Company
P.O. Box 6287, Grand Rapids, MI 49516-6287

Second printing, December 1997

Printed in the United States of America

Library of Congress Cataloging-in-Publication Data

Galloway, Dale E.
    The small group book : the practical guide for nurturing
Christians and building churches / Dale Galloway with Kathi
Mills.
       p.   cm.
    ISBN 0-8007-5570-7 (pbk.)
    1. Church group work. 2. Church growth. 3. Church
development, New. I. Mills, Kathi, 1948– . II. Title.
BV652.2.G35   1995
253'.7—dc20   95-2892

For current information about all releases from
Baker Book House, visit our web site:
           http://www.bakerbooks.com/

The Small Group Book

Contents

Introduction

The Vision

On October 14, 1972, New Hope Community Church was launched—not at the beautiful, big campus where it now resides, but at a drive-in theater in Portland, Oregon. However, long before that first service, my wife, Margi, and I were hosting a small group in our home—the nucleus of people who were to become the fledgling congregation of New Hope—looking forward to the day when we would see the fulfillment of the vision God had given us. A few weeks after that first service, I stood on the roof of the drive-in snack shack and shared that vision with the already growing congregation.

That vision was of a three-thousand-seat sanctuary with a one hundred-foot lighted cross rising above its roof, nestled against a lush, green hillside overlooking one of the busiest freeways in metropolitan Portland. That church would stand as a beacon to draw thousands of lost, unchurched, hurting people to a place of new life, new hope, new dreams, and fresh visions of their own, a place where they could come and receive unconditional love, acceptance, and forgiveness. Because of our own involvement in small-group ministry, Margi and I had long since come to believe that effective evangelism and ministry takes place in small groups. I was therefore determined that this church would be built on and around the concept of small-group ministry. That was the vision I conveyed to our congregation, and because of my certainty that this vision was of God and not of my own making, it didn't matter what the pessimists and naysayers declared. I knew it would come to pass.

And it did. High against the green hillside overlooking a busy freeway and a huge shopping mall, that one-hundred-foot cross now proclaims the truth that when God gives us a vision, he also gives us the means to see that vision become a reality.

The Ministry of Small Groups

As our congregation continued to grow at a phenomenal rate, Margi and I were overwhelmed—not only with joy and gratitude that God was bringing people in, but with the awesome responsibility of ministering to such a vast number of people. We wanted so desperately to maintain personal contact with each and every member of our flock, but as that flock increased, our realization of the impossibility of such a task also increased.

In time, however, God brought us to a point where we knew that to maintain personal ministry within the congregation, the small-group ministry I had long envisioned with lay pastors to oversee manageable numbers of people was the only possible way to accomplish what we believed God had assigned us to do. We also knew that our small-group ministry had to be more than just an "appendage" to the other ministries within New Hope's structure; it had to be the heartbeat of the ministry, the center out of which all other ministries of the church flowed.

It took time, and we made a lot of mistakes along the way, but God has been faithful to bless and multiply our efforts. We now minister to approximately five thousand people each week in small-group settings.

I believe that no church with more than fifty members can be effective in pastoral care without enlisting and enabling lay people to do the daily work of that care. And that is why I have written this book. It is also why I have recorded a tape series on small groups and why I teach seminars on the subject all across the country. The absolute necessity of small-group ministry within the church is a concept that must be understood and implemented by pastors and church leaders if we are ever to effectively equip the church for ministry in these last days.

Changing Tradition to Meet the Needs of the '90s

And yet in spite of the need for small groups, there is still much resistance to this type of ministry. Why is that? There are many reasons, which we will explore in depth throughout this book, but one of the toughest to overcome is the "seven last words" of the church: "We've never done it that way before." (Actually, small-group ministry, particularly meeting in individual homes, goes all the way back to the early church and is modeled in the Book of Acts. But for some reason, some people do not see the early church model as relevant today.)

And so we insist on continuing to do things the way Grandma did them—whether they work or not. The church seems determined to ignore the fact that we live in an ever-changing world. This is fine if the reason for resisting change is because the change is not scriptural. But if the reason for resistance is because we just don't want to try anything new, then we've become stuck in a tradition that is no longer life producing.

Why Every Church Needs Small Groups

The seven last words of the church—we've never done it that way before—call to mind some of the last words of Jesus as he hung on the cross: "Father, forgive them, for they do not know what they are doing" (Luke 23:34). Those who are opposed to small-group ministry simply do not understand what they are opposing and why this type of ministry is so necessary. There are five basic reasons why every church needs small groups:

1. They provide multiple points of entry into the church.
2. They provide a very effective form of evangelism.
3. They are the only way to truly care for people.
4. They accelerate the spiritual growth of individuals and the church.
5. They properly shift the work of the church to the people and fulfill Ephesians 4.

Caring for One Another

One hot August night a few years ago, my phone rang. It was one of our lay pastors who said, "Pastor, I'm over at the Joneses' home [not their real name] and they're in desperate need. Our district pastor is on vacation. Can you come over?"

By the time I arrived, the house was full of people—most of them members of the small TLC (Tender Loving Care) group to which the Jones family belonged. When I learned what had happened, I was dumbfounded. It was one of those times you just sit with people, pray with them, and do your best to comfort them, but you really can't think of anything very meaningful to say.

The Joneses were watching the six o'clock news on television when a picture of their daughter came on the screen.

Their daughter was grown and lived with her army husband in another part of the country. She had pretended to be pregnant for some time, even going so far as to wear maternity clothes. Then she had stalked a pregnant woman, watching and following her to the army hospital. When the pregnant woman came out of the hospital, the Joneses' daughter kidnapped her and took her out to the desert, where she strangled her and cut the baby out of her stomach. Miraculously, the baby survived.

Can you imagine the shock and pain of that couple as this story about their own child unfolded right in front of their eyes? Can you see why it was almost impossible to find the right words to say at a time like that? And yet even after I left, the members of their TLC group stayed on, some of them into the night. Others returned the next day with food, love, and support.

Soon after that evening at the Joneses' home, I went on vacation. When I returned, I asked their district pastor how they were doing.

"Pastor," he replied, "you should have been here on Sunday. When the Joneses arrived, their entire TLC group flocked to their side. They hugged them and sat with them throughout the service, even going down front with them at prayer time. It was beautiful."

I don't personally give that kind of care to the people at New Hope. I can't. There are simply too many people.

I can be sitting in a restaurant with my wife when someone comes up and says, "Hello, Pastor."

"Hello," I respond. "How are you?"

When they're gone, I ask Margi, "Was that a member of our church?"

Truthfully, however, it wasn't much better when the church was small. Even with fifty or one hundred members, I couldn't give that kind of care. But a small group of eight to ten people can—and they do, as the Joneses' case so clearly illustrates.

Small-group ministry is not an option if people are to be cared for, nurtured, and equipped for ministry. And if people aren't prepared, they can't be about the work of the ministry, which is evangelizing, discipling, and caring for others.

I believe in small groups. The leadership at New Hope Community Church believes in small groups. With all my heart, I pray this book will convey to you our passion for small-group ministry. More than that, I pray it will give you the practical answers you need to totally integrate small-group ministry into the very life-fiber of your own church—whatever its size.

Why Small Groups?

When Jesus walked this earth two thousand years ago, he was usually surrounded by faithful followers, as well as the curious and those who hoped to see—or experience—a miracle. Those faithful followers were referred to as "disciples." Before Jesus left this earth to return to heaven, he told his followers to "go and make disciples" (see Matt. 28:18–20). In other words, the disciples were to reproduce—disciples making disciples. This command of Jesus is referred to as the Great Commission.

There is nothing more exciting than to be in a great evangelistic crusade where multitudes are "saved" or "born again" as they open their hearts and lives to the lordship of Jesus Christ. This, of course, is the first part of the Great Commission. We can't become disciples without first being converts. But the church's work doesn't end there. In fact, it is where the work truly begins.

At the point when we are converted, we are as "saved" as we will ever be; if we were to drop dead at that moment, we would go straight to heaven. But we would not have had time to become disciples. A disciple is a "disciplined one," someone who has learned from a designated teacher by example, instruction, and experience over a period of time. As a result of discipleship, the life of the student is changed.

And this is what needs to happen in the church. Most churches today are filled with broken, bruised, inexperienced converts but few healthy, dedicated disciples. That's why it is so hard to find enough competent, qualified, and willing leaders to begin and maintain needed ministries. Converts are simply not yet qualified to lead. Only a disciple who has had "on-the-job" training with a more mature and experienced disciple is qualified—and confident enough—to lead others.

At New Hope, we believe that the best and most effective place to train or disciple a future leader is in a small group. We believe it is vital to get new members involved in small groups as quickly as possible. In small groups their sense of "family" is established, their personal needs are met, and their potential for ministry is released. It is simply impossible for these things to happen in the context of large weekend celebration services, as exciting and enjoyable as those may be.

For a large percentage of our members, involvement in a small group is a given, because they come into the church through small-group ministry and are later assimilated into the weekend celebration services. This is a simpler and much more effective transition than trying to convince people whose church mindset consists of once a week on Sunday mornings to become involved in a small-group experience. In fact, over the years we have observed that those who come into the church via Sunday morning services and do not subsequently become involved in small groups are the ones we ultimately lose. Why?

Because they simply don't feel connected, cared for, or needed. The chances of these people moving into true discipleship are slim.

New Hope—A New Model

New Hope Community Church is currently the largest small-group driven, or lay-leader driven, church in North America, and we are extremely grateful to hold that distinction, even temporarily. But being a trailblazer isn't always easy. Years ago I decided I would have to break the mold if I was ever to do what I knew God had called me to do. And so I looked all over the world for ideas on how to develop a great church. It was in Dr. Cho's church in Korea that I found a model I thought would be helpful in my search for a way to establish a church where the pastoral care needs of the congregation would be met.

Consequently I decided to transplant to the U.S. as much as I understood of the Cho model, despite the naysayers who said it couldn't be done. I doggedly pursued a vision of establishing lay pastors to care for a limited number of small-group members in home cells, as well as to perform pastoral calls and visits within the group. That way I knew we would have enough lay leaders to cover the pastoral care needs of the congregation, whether I was there or not. The fulfillment of that vision would release me to be away from the church for periods of time without having to be concerned about whether or not the people's needs were being met.

As I pursued my vision, I encountered various problems stemming from the fact that I was operating almost alone in a virtual leadership vacuum in the U.S. Whole denominations were experimenting with small-group ministries and rejecting them for a variety of reasons. But while they were saying it couldn't be done, we were beginning to see progress in our pursuit of excellence in pastoral care through sharing the burden of that care with trained lay pastors. In essence, I don't really see New Hope as a model of small-group ministry as much as a model of lay-pastor ministry, with small groups as an important component.

The Importance of Leadership

As I've said before, New Hope's beginnings were humble; it was eight years before we had our first building, which was more of a multipurpose building than a sanctuary. It was our custom to serve communion on the first Sunday of every month. We set it up on a table where people could come up, take the elements, and then go back to their seats. The entire procedure was dependent on getting the first person started right so that everyone would follow in the proper order. The system worked wonderfully most of the time. However, there were exceptions.

One Sunday morning, everyone stood. The first person took a step and everyone followed him. Unfortunately, that first person was headed for the bathroom. The entire first row followed him. It wasn't until the second and third rows were stacked up behind them that they figured out they were headed in the wrong direction!

Is leadership important? You better believe it! Without leaders in the church who know who they are in Christ and where the church is going, you end up with a leadership vacuum—and anything but good goes into that vacuum. Churches desperately need strong leadership.

All church growth begins in the mind, heart, and soul of a chosen man or woman who will become the leader of the church. As that leader's vision is shared with others, they also become a part of the fulfilling of that vision, regardless of their title or position. Leadership is about influence, not titles.

When I was first out of seminary, I thought it was important to be addressed as "Reverend Dale Galloway." I soon learned it didn't matter what people called me. It was influence that mattered. I only have leadership as I have influence with people. In order to take people from point A to point B, we must know how to influence them. Often that means being able to influence the influencers.

This book will not just give you tools for ministry, but will lift your vision, teach you how to lead people through influence, and help others catch the vision and dream your dream. It is a book about shared ministry. I believe there is someone reading this book who will dream a new dream about small-group ministry and the far-reaching impact and possibilities of lay leadership that will take you far beyond anything we've done at New Hope. For some of you, this may be a first-time vision, for others, a renewal of a vision. Everything begins with a vision. Nothing will happen anywhere—including the church—until someone lays hold of a God-given vision and determines to pursue it. Your life—and your church—will never go any higher than the vision of your leaders.

Meeting the Needs of the Church

George Gallup, a very fine Episcopal layman, found that 70 percent of Americans say the church is not meeting their needs. (What does that say about church leadership?) When he asked what these needs were, six were mentioned most often:

1. To believe life is meaningful and has purpose
2. To have a sense of community and deeper relationships
3. To be appreciated and respected
4. To be listened to and heard
5. To grow in faith
6. To receive practical help in developing a mature faith

These are needs that must be met if a convert is to become a disciple. All six of these needs are met in small-group ministry.

One of the things that most excites me about small-group ministry is that it fulfills the "one another" principle of the New Testament. Take a moment to read through the Scripture references listed in the following table (from *Prepare Your Church for the Future,* by Carl George, pp. 129–31) and you'll see what I mean. I am aware of no other setting in the daily life of the church that affords this opportunity.

The "One Another's" of the New Testament

1. "... be at peace with each other" (Mark 9:50b).
2. "... wash one another's feet" (John 13:14).
3. "A new command I give you: Love one another" (John 13:34a).
4. "As I have loved you, so you must love one another" (John 13:34b).
5. "... love one another" (John 13:35).
6. "Love each other as I have loved you" (John 15:12).
7. "This is my command: Love each other" (John 15:17).
8. "Be devoted to one another in brotherly love" (Rom. 12:10a).
9. "Honor one another above yourselves" (Rom. 12:10b).
10. "Live in harmony with one another" (Rom. 12:16a).
11. "... love one another ..." (Rom. 13:8).
12. "Stop passing judgment on one another" (Rom. 14:13a).
13. "Accept one another, then, just as Christ accepted you ..." (Rom. 15:7).
14. "... instruct one another" (Rom. 15:14).
15. "Greet one another with a holy kiss" (Rom. 16:16a).
16. "... when you come together to eat, wait for each other" (1 Cor. 11:33).
17. "... have equal concern for each other" (1 Cor. 12:25).

18. "Greet one another with a holy kiss" (1 Cor. 16:20b).
19. "Greet one another with a holy kiss" (2 Cor. 13:12).
20. ". . . serve one another in love" (Gal. 5:13b).
21. "If you keep on biting and devouring each other . . . you will be destroyed by each other" (Gal. 5:15).
22. "Let us not become conceited, provoking and envying each other" (Gal. 5:26).
23. "Carry each other's burdens . . ." (Gal. 6:2).
24. ". . . be patient, bearing with one another in love" (Eph. 4:2).
25. "Be kind and compassionate to one another . . ." (Eph. 4:32).
26. ". . . forgiving each other just as in Christ God forgave you" (Eph. 4:32).
27. "Speak to one another with psalms, hymns and spiritual songs" (Eph. 5:19).
28. "Submit to one another out of reverence for Christ" (Eph. 5:21).
29. ". . . in humility consider others better than yourselves" (Phil. 2:3).
30. "Do not lie to each other . . ." (Col. 3:9).
31. "Bear with each other . . ." (Col. 3:13a).
32. ". . . forgive whatever grievances you may have against one another" (Col. 3:13a).
33. "Let the word of Christ dwell in you richly as you teach . . ." (Col. 3:16a).
34. ". . . admonish one another with all wisdom . . ." (Col. 3:16b).
35. "May the Lord make your love increase and overflow for each other . . ." (1 Thess. 3:12).
36. ". . . love each other" (1 Thess. 4:9).
37. ". . . encourage each other . . ." (1 Thess. 4:18).
38. ". . . encourage one another . . ." (1 Thess. 5:11).
39. ". . . build each other up . . ." (1 Thess. 5:11).
40. "Encourage one another daily . . ." (Heb. 3:13).

Where Do Small Groups Fit in the Church?

Basically, there are three types of small-group systems represented in America: the appendage system, the incorporated or department system, and the totally integrated system. Choosing the right type of system is key to the success of small-group ministry within any church.

The Appendage System

The first system—the appendage system—is a system where some lay person has initiated a small group without any support or recognition from church leadership. The group is not mentioned from the pulpit or in the weekly bulletin or newsletter. If the pastor is aware of the group, he or she may mention it to someone, but does not actively promote it. No leadership training is offered within the church, so the group stands or falls on its own.

The Incorporated or Department System

The second system—the incorporated or department system—is the traditional system established in the majority of churches across the country. It consists of departments such as youth departments, music departments, and outreach departments. When someone begins to push for small-group ministry, the usual response of these churches is to create a small-group department to be overseen by a small-group pastor. This is the way most churches in America view small-group ministry. In fact, I get many calls from churches all over the country asking me to recommend a good small-group minister.

Now much good can be done by implementing this system, but it has built-in limits. For example, when I came back from Korea the first time, I was so excited about prayer ministry, I said to one of the people on my staff, "I want you to be in charge of prayer at our church." One year later I had to reverse my "prayer department" thinking because I found out that all my other pastors had checked out on prayer! They didn't go to any of the prayer events because they figured they had other ministry activities to oversee.

What happened was that we had become departmentalized to the point of having a prayer department with no one else involved in praying except the one assigned to oversee that department. The same thing can happen with small-group ministry if we allow ourselves to become compartmentalized in our thinking.

The Totally Integrated System

The third system—the totally integrated system—is the one we use at New Hope. In a totally integrated system, small groups are involved in every aspect of the church. In fact, they are the structure of the church. New Hope's leaders believe in small-group ministry; they support it because they've caught the vision for it. Small-group ministry is not just another ministry we do. It is the blood vessel system of the whole body of the church. We have become a totally integrated system.

In our training seminars, lay or staff people from other churches will come up to me and say things like, "Our senior pastor isn't here today. Can we still implement what you're teaching into our church?" I assure them that they can, but I also caution them that their church will never go as far or reach as high in small-group ministry as they could if their senior pastor were to catch the vision and it became his or her heart and dream. No matter who introduces small-group ministry into a church, that ministry will only go as far as the senior pastor's vision for it. The people will watch the senior pastor to see if small-group ministry is important to him or her, because what's important to the senior pastor is important to the people.

I'm not ashamed to admit that I intentionally stack our church board. I do everything I can to influence the influencers to get people elected to our board who are small-group leaders, people who are in small groups, and people who believe 100 percent in small-group ministry. Why? Because if I die tonight and someone else comes to pastor my church, I want to make sure small-group ministry continues.

Most-Asked Questions about Small Groups

When Should Groups Meet?

One of the questions I'm asked quite often is, "Do you group people in a certain time or place for small groups?" The answer is no. We believe in grouping people together anywhere, anytime we can. The only thing we have to decide is whether groups will meet during the day or in the evening, which day(s), and how often. We have chosen to break out of the space/time box and have said to our lay leaders, "You have your group at the best time to get your people together." We now have groups on every day of the week, morning, afternoon, and evening. No one can say there isn't a convenient time to attend a group meeting.

What Qualities Should Small-Group Leaders Have?

Another question I am often asked is, "What kind of spiritual gifts do you look for in prospective leaders of these small groups?" First, decide if the leader is more of a teacher-type or a facilitator. Ninety-five percent of our lay leaders are facilitators because facilitators can be reproduced much easier than teachers. Of course, if a person has the gift of teaching and wants to have that kind of group, we give them the green light to do so.

Do You Assign People to Groups?

A key question is, "Do you assign people to groups? If not, who recruits them?" Have you ever tried to assign people to groups? If you have, you know it doesn't work. You can try to divide up your people by zone or area, assign an elder to each area, and tell the people which group to attend on a particular day at a given time. It all looks good on a map or chart on the wall. But in reality, it will be a mess. People will go where they feel drawn, not where they're assigned. Besides, maps and charts don't build groups—leaders do.

As a pastor, I try to do everything I can to convince people to get involved in a group. But assigning them just doesn't work. I have found that like attracts like, and people will often try several different groups before they find the one that "fits." What we do in practice is say to someone, "Now here's a group close to where you live, and we think you'd really enjoy it. We'll give your name to the group's leader, who will then call you. But if you feel you don't fit in that group, we'll work with you to find one where you do." We keep matching people with people until they connect.

How Do You Manage Leaders?

What about supervision? What kind of coaching should be provided for lay leaders? I believe the most important element of effective leadership is encouragement. If my pastoral staff encourages the lay leadership, the lay leadership will in turn encourage the people in their groups. People who become discouraged will drop out of a group and out of leadership if they aren't supervised with encouragement. If you have a discouraged leader, give them a little time and a lot of encouragement and they'll do just fine. We will discuss the elements of effective supervision in detail in chapter 6.

How Do You Avoid Divisions and Splintering?

I've had many pastors ask me if there isn't a certain amount of danger of divisiveness and splintering with this kind of decentralized system. They ask me if I'm afraid people will become disloyal or turn against me. Amazingly enough, I've never had that happen. I believe that's because of the accountability we have built into the system.

After our lay pastors complete their initial training, they fill out a commitment sheet, promising to take training every week, to live by what we require of lay pastors, and to fill out a report sheet every week. Actually, there are two report sheets—one for their own personal ministry for Christ, the second for the group meeting.

Of course there is always someone who says, "I don't like to fill out reports." We explain to them that we understand they don't like to do it, but they have to give the report to the senior pastor, then to the board, if they are going to be a part of lay leadership. This system helps us work together as a team. If there are those who feel they cannot abide by our standards, then they are free to start their own appendage groups, away from our accountability or involvement. The choice is theirs.

This is how we effectively weed out rebels. Rebellious people will not want to play on the team. They won't want to come to training or fill out reports. And they usually drop out of commitment down the road. Accountability to commitment is essential. The ones who don't want to be accountable to come to training or fill out reports are the same ones who, later on, want to be the Lone Ranger instead of a part of the team.

It may be that some of you have small groups already but no accountability in place. What are you going to do? If I were in your place, decided accountability was important, and wanted to implement it, I would create a "two-track" system—one track being the leaders already in place and the second being new leaders who start off with training and accountability in place. Give yourself two or three years to phase out those in the old track who do not want to change to training and accountability. During this time you will be bringing in the new track. Encourage the old track people to come into the new track, but if they won't, they will eventually fade away.

Sharing the Burdens of Ministry

In conclusion, there are two key principles that we must lay hold of if we are to incorporate successful small-group ministry into our churches and, in doing so, help fulfill the Great Commission. These principles are: *give up control* and *give up control.*

First, for you pastors, you will never have an effective small-group ministry or lay-driven ministry if you are not willing to give up some control and practice what we call "shared ministry" with lay people. I know that's easier said than done, but it is absolutely necessary. We must learn to share ministry, to give it away, to allow things to go on when we're not there, to trust other people to run ministries, and to continue to give up control so ministry can grow beyond us. The care of the people must shift from the pastor caring for people to the people caring for people—disciples making disciples. After all, that's what Jesus commissioned us to do. For a lot of churches, this is revolutionary thinking. It must happen, however, if we are to break out of the old ways of thinking that have restricted us and move on into the growth God wants us to have.

The second principle is that the church board or council (or whoever runs things in your church) must also give up control over details in day-to-day operations. They must begin to allow pastors of different ministries to make the daily decisions that must be made in order for their ministries to run smoothly and grow effectively.

In summary, both the senior pastor and the church board must be willing to give up control in certain areas in order to enable growth within the church. It's a tough thing to do, but we'll examine some practical ways of accomplishing this in the next chapter.

Remember, it was Jesus who commissioned us to go out and make disciples who, in turn, will make disciples and build *his* church—not our church.

Breaking Out of the Boxes

Slightly more than twenty years ago, the dream of New Hope Community Church was launched. Even though at that time we had only one small group, which my wife and I led in our home, I talked about my vision. "This will be a church that will have hundreds of lay pastor-led small groups throughout the metropolitan area, with ministry happening every day of the week."

It was a pretty extravagant vision for such humble beginnings. We had come early that first day—as we did each Sunday morning after that—to clean up the trash that had been left on the field of the drive-in theater the night before. We had a man inside the snack shack who operated the sound system. He had never been to church before, so he was unfamiliar with the songs we sang. Invariably, he'd play the wrong song and my wife would have to stop singing and say to him, "That's the wrong song. Please turn to the other side." As I said, it was a humble, humble beginning, but I've always been a firm believer in Proverbs

29:18, which reads, "Where there is no vision, the people perish" (KJV). I knew if I could cast the vision, and the people could catch it, we would move forward and see that vision become a reality.

Casting the Vision

But it was not to happen without challenges. That very first week, as I stood on the roof and proclaimed the vision God had given me, there was a man sitting in his car, his wife beside him and his dog in the back seat. They were sitting there, drinking their coffee while I described this beautiful church we would someday have, and he poked his wife and said, "That guy's crazy! I think I'll keep coming here every Sunday morning just so I can laugh at him!"

He wasn't the only one who thought I was "dreaming too big." Even as the vision took hold in the hearts of the people and God led us to the very spot above the I-205 freeway where we would build the church, the naysayers were there.

The property was just what God had promised us it would be—a beautiful spot on a lush green hillside, adjacent to an exit from a major freeway, and overlooking the freeway as well as the largest shopping mall in Oregon! Even before we poured the foundation, I could look at that spot and see that three-thousand-seat sanctuary, with the one-hundred-foot lighted cross towering above it, calling people to New Hope. The architect, however, tried his best to convince me that it just couldn't be done.

"Impossible," he said when I described the lighted cross. "It's too windy up here on this hill. It simply can't be done."

Now when someone tells me something can't be done, the hair kind of stands up on the back of my neck, especially when I know God has given me the vision. And so I said to the architect, "It must be done. God has given me the vision. Therefore, there has to be a way to do it."

Well, he came back when he had designed the building with a picture of the ugliest cross you could ever imagine! It was propped up on both sides and it looked just horrible. It wouldn't have been an inspiration to anyone. "That's not it," I told him. "That is not the cross that God has shown me will be atop our building. It must be one hundred feet high, illuminated, and free standing."

Apart from our running disagreement over this cross, the architect and I got along rather well. He was, in fact, a great architect; he simply didn't share our vision. Finally, however, I told him that we could not give him any more money until he found a way to design the cross exactly as God had shown us it would be—a cross that people could see for miles along the freeway.

The architect frowned, took a deep breath, and left. One week later, he came back with a design for the most beautiful, illuminated, free-standing, *108*-foot cross imaginable! We were ecstatic.

Fruit of the Vision

We'd no sooner got the building completed and that cross mounted above it than a man named John came driving down the freeway toward us. That very day his wife had left him, and he was contemplating suicide. Then he came into view of the cross. As he saw it, a spark of hope began to flicker in his heart. Could this be an answer for him, he wondered. Could there possibly be something left to live for?

He got off at the exit and drove into our parking lot. That night our singles ministry was meeting. John walked into the sanctuary and sat down. At the end of the service, the pastor gave an invitation to receive Christ. John came forward and knelt. Lay pastors came down and met with him and prayed for him. The following night they brought him to a support group where they surrounded him with love and care. He attended another support group the next night. I finally met him the following Sunday morning. By then, the process of healing had already begun.

I remember seeing John a few months later. He was standing over in a corner praying for someone else who had come in broken and alone. "Oh God," I thought, "what if we'd given up on the dream? What if we'd decided the cross didn't matter?" There are many things we do in church that really don't matter—but following through on the vision God has given you is not one of them!

I pray that as you read this book, God will renew your vision—or give you a brand new one—of what can happen when you work with lay people and set them free in small-group ministry. Nothing is impossible if we catch God's dream and vision that he has for us right now!

Making the Vision Reality

But if we are ever to see those dreams and visions become reality, we must be willing to break out of what I call "The Twelve Growth-Restrictive Boxes." Let's look at those boxes and see how we can do just that.

Box #1—Small Thinking

Actually, I like to refer to this box as "stinking thinking." Let me tell you why. I live in a large metropolitan area of about a million people. In my book *20/20 Vision*, which has now been circulated throughout the world, I tell a story of a man named Bob. Bob is a Christian repairman who went to the home of one of our members. In the course of their conversation, they began to talk about their churches. The member of New Hope described our outreach ministry through lay-led small groups, explaining that these groups had resulted in a membership explosion with 80 percent of our members never having been in church before. Bob shook his head.

"Well, I'm sure glad I belong to a nice small church of about fifty members," he said. "I wouldn't like it if it was any bigger."

If the pastor of that church shares Bob's vision, Bob can rest assured that his "nice small church" will never grow any larger than it is right now. What a sad commentary on what the church is all about! Here he was, attending church in the middle of a large metropolitan area where, within fifteen minutes of that church, there were literally thousands of unchurched people, people who desperately needed Christ but would certainly not be welcome to come to Bob's church to find him. Pathetic! Stinking thinking.

People never grow beyond their vision. Dare to enlarge your vision! Dare to break out of that puny, small-thinking box! Someone has said, "You will become as small as your controlling desire; as great as your dominant aspiration." Think about it. What is your controlling desire, your dominant aspiration? What is your vision? Whatever it is, I believe God wants to enlarge it.

Box #2—Sunday Only

So many churches are locked into the restrictive idea that they can only have church on Sunday. Ministry needs to take place seven days a week, not only on the church premises, but wherever members are. The successful church of the future will be the one with ministry going on around the clock throughout the week.

I remember sitting in a church growth seminar at Dr. Bob Schuller's church more than twenty years ago. In fact, I think we were up in the tower on the thirteenth floor. My wife and I were sitting together. That day, in a prophetic manner, Dr. Schuller said, "Someday someone here will build a greater church. That church will be a seven-day-a-week church." And that is the description of our church here at New Hope, with groups meeting throughout the week. So much wonderful ministry is taking place because we have broken out of that Sunday-only box.

Box #3—One Service Only

I believe that one of the first ways you begin to break out to become a larger church is when you move to multiple services. As long as people have to control everything and see everyone at the same time, we're trapped in that one-service box.

There is a church in our community that had grown to about five hundred members. Their facilities were filled to capacity, and they knew if they were to grow any larger, they would have to make a change. The pastor suggested, "Let's go to a second service. We can have twice as many people in this building and double our resources." But he was voted down. They sold their building and tried to relocate, but got into a terrible financial mess. Now membership is dropping rapidly, and their vision is being lost in the shuffle—all because they refused to break out of that one-service-only box.

In my observation and experience, when a church decides to break out of that growth-restrictive box and go to multiple services, healthy growth is the result. Even when we were still meeting in a drive-in theater, we had to go to two services almost immediately. It was a good move, because we never had time to get stuck in that one-service-only thinking.

Box #4—The Church as a Building

I am so glad that God didn't allow us to have a building of our own for the first eight years of New Hope's existence. During that eight years we were "nomads." In addition to meeting at the drive-in theater, we met in every other type of building imaginable. And just about the time we'd get comfortable in one of them, God would move us someplace else. It was during that time we *really* learned that the church is people, not a building.

The church-as-a-building box is a dangerous one. Once locked into that type of thinking, it is almost impossible to imagine ministry taking place anywhere other than in the building. What a limited concept of ministry! The building is nothing more than an instrument to be used by people ministering to people. When we begin to understand that, ministry can continue beyond the building to wherever people are.

Box #5—*Sunday School Only*

There are certainly some churches who have made great progress through Sunday school ministry, but we cannot allow ourselves to think that Sunday school is the only way to educate and disciple people—as I would hope you are learning by reading this book. Yes, I believe Sunday school is important. I also believe Sunday school is an effective ministry tool. But I do not believe it is the only tool.

I believe God wants to group people in countless ways—through support groups that minister to people with common needs, small groups designed to disciple new believers, groups to teach and extend ministry, groups of people called to a common task, groups meeting in certain geographical areas, and groups geared toward the elderly, singles, youth, and the creatively gifted. The list is endless! If we limit ourselves to thinking that Sunday school is the only way, we will automatically limit ourselves by time, space, and location.

Box #6—All Groups Meet on the Same Night

So many pastors limit their church's growth by the erroneous thinking that if they're going to institute small-group ministry, all the groups must meet on the same night (or in the same building or at the same time of day). I say, let the people who lead the groups decide when and where to meet. Otherwise, not only are pastors restricting their church's growth, they are restricting the people's vision for how important small-group ministry really is.

If you allow the small-group leaders to decide on meeting times and places, they will automatically choose the time and place best suited to the needs of the group. After all, aren't the people who attend the group the ones who should most benefit from the group's existence? If someone has a vision to start a group for young mothers and, after speaking to some of the young mothers regarding the group, discovers that the majority feel a midmorning, midweek meeting time would best suit their needs, why not allow them to meet at that time? It's this type of versatility that enables small groups to minister in a way that the weekend celebration service simply cannot.

Box #7—Pastor-Controlled Ministries

Pastors, we've got to allow God to enlarge our vision! We've got to break out of the box manufactured and perpetuated by our own insecurities and begin giving ministry away.

You see, if we as pastors are not open to shared ministry because we feel we must control all the ministries in our church, we're not going to get very big because we'll never grow any larger than our own arms can reach. In a real sense, we must give up control of ministries in order to break out of this restrictive box and release unlimited growth in our churches. Simply put, if we aren't willing to let go, we will never see that growth.

Box #8—Board Control

Churches are so limited when they have a board that is ultra-controlling and won't let the decision makers—the leaders—make any decisions! If a pastor has to call a board meeting every time a decision needs to be made about ministry, that church's growth is going to be severely limited. If board members feel they need to decide on every little thing that happens, every minute detail, the ministry growth and potential of the church will never be reached.

As an example, the children's pastor at New Hope, Clara Olson, knows everything about running a nursery. And she does her job well. I, on the other hand, know nothing about running a nursery. A young couple from our church told me recently that after visiting our church the first time, they continued to come back each week for one primary reason—the woman in the nursery loved their baby. That was important to them, and it's important to me. I can trust Clara completely to see that the children who are brought to our children's ministry are loved, cared for, and nurtured.

Now wouldn't it be ridiculous for me to meet with the church board to decide how the nursery should be run, rather than trusting a qualified person who already knows how to run a nursery to make those decisions herself? Of course it would be ridiculous—and a waste of time, at that. Our board makes themselves available to answer questions or help out if needed, but otherwise they trust proven leaders to do their jobs.

What I see in many churches are assigned lay people running all these "things," carrying out "assignments," but not involved in ministry because they have no sense of ownership. We need to shift that paradigm to where lay people are in ministry at the grass roots. Sure, we still need *accountability*, but we must also recognize *ability* in lay leaders to make the day-by-day, and sometimes moment-by-moment, decisions that need to be made. As a church grows, the pastoral team—both paid staff and lay leaders—need to be free to make many ministry decisions.

Box #9—Super Stars

Pastor, you can do anything!

If we allow ourselves to buy into that lie, we've just bought our own failure. It's a partnership between clergy and lay people that leads to the fulfillment of a church's God-given vision.

I love what I once heard Carl George, an expert on small-group ministry, say about partnership between clergy and laity. According to George, in his church over the years the gap between lay people and clergy has disappeared, and they're all just partnering together in ministry. No more super stars!

Remember, we'll never live up to super-star expectations. No one can.

Box #10—Assistant Pastor

Now this is just my own little thing, but I don't like the title assistant pastor. That sounds to me like I'm bringing someone in to do the things I don't want to do. Although we all need people to help us with details, I don't want someone cleaning up after me. When I bring someone on staff, I look for three things:

- Someone who can do something I can't. Otherwise, why would I need the person?
- Someone who sees the ministry as equipping and training lay people for the ministry. This person must be committed to reproducing him- or herself through other people's lives because then when that pastor leaves, there's still going to be a lot of ministry going on.

- Someone who can be placed over entire area(s) of ministry. This must be someone to whom I can confidently say, "Here, this area of ministry is yours. You dream it. You build it. You make it as big as the vision God gives you."

Box #11—Comfort Zones

I know that old shoes are more comfortable than new ones simply because we've worn them so long. They "fit" our feet. They feel good. But if we limit ourselves to wearing only old, comfortable shoes, we're going to miss out on many beautiful new shoes that might be custom-made just for us!

Dr. Schuller used to tell a story about a man who went fishing every chance he got. He really loved to fish! But one day, no matter how hard he tried, he just couldn't catch any fish. To make matters worse, he could see a guy in a boat nearby who was catching a fish every few minutes. One thing that seemed rather odd to him, however, was that the man kept throwing the biggest fish back, keeping only the small ones in his boat. Finally, the frustrated fisherman couldn't take it anymore.

"Hey," he yelled. "How come you're throwing all the big fish back?"

The other fisherman reached under the seat in his boat and pulled out a small frying pan. "Because they won't fit in the pan," he answered.

Comfort zones. How many times have we thrown out the big fish in the vision God gave us because they didn't fit in our comfortable "frying pan"? Maybe it's time to break out of our comfort zone and get a bigger pan.

Box #12—The Seven Last Words of the Church

We've never done it that way before. These are the seven last words of the church—tragic words, heartbreaking words, growth-stifling words, the death knell of a vision.

We live in a changing world, and if we are going to fulfill the Great Commission, as Jesus told us to do, we must
learn to adapt our ministry to a relevant form. If we are
unwilling to do so, we are in effect inscribing the name
"Ichabod"—meaning "the glory has departed"—over our
church door. And when the glory of God's presence is
gone, death is already upon us, even if we are too blind to
recognize it.

Nothing happens without a vision. If we are ever to
break out of these growth-restrictive boxes, we must pursue the vision that God has given us, without compromise
and without regard to those who say it can't be done.

Hebrews 11:1 says, "Now faith is being sure of what we
hope for and certain of what we do not see." To paraphrase
that verse, "Faith is vision . . . and vision is seeing something before it exists."

Ask God to sharpen and enlarge your vision . . . and then
trust him to enable you to fulfill it.

3

Growing
with Small Groups

It happened slightly more than twenty-five years ago—
one of the most frustrating experiences I have ever had
in the ministry.

I had just come from starting a new church in a suburb
of Columbus, Ohio. There I'd seen evangelism in action
and many people reached for Christ. I had come to a very
old, established, traditional church, which didn't seem in
the least concerned that they hadn't reached anyone for
Christ in years.

I was about twenty-six at the time—young, energetic,
and raring to go. I'll never forget my first board meeting
when I began to share the great ideas I had on evangelism
and how we were going to reach people with the gospel.
Every idea I came up with they squelched. The next board
meeting the following month was even worse. That's when
I realized I was hitting the wall of tradition. What I didn't
yet understand was that they had their own "private"

meetings before they ever came to the board meetings. It was at these private meetings that the decisions were actually made about what they were and were not going to do in that church.

So here I was, a young, eager pastor with a church that hadn't had any new people come in for years, a church that was content with seeing the same people, week after week, month after month, year after year. It was a dead church—and I was beginning to think I would die with it. That's when I called my father, who was a church administrator as well as my close and trusted friend. He cautioned me to move slowly and trust God for a way to bring life into this dead church.

During that time I began to read many books and do a lot of research on how to reach people for Christ. It was then that I came across some material about small groups. As I read the material, I thought, *This is it! This is a wonderful idea! I believe this would work!*

So I called my father again and he said, "Son, I agree with you. If you're ever going to grow a healthy church of any size, you've got to have small groups."

Once again, I presented my plan to the board. Once again, my idea was squelched. In fact, I couldn't get anyone at the church interested in the concept of small-group ministry. They felt that the traditional Wednesday night prayer meeting they already had was enough midweek ministry.

Actually, these Wednesday night prayer meetings consisted of about twenty people—roughly 10 percent of the congregation—who showed up every Wednesday evening, scattered out all over the sanctuary, and talked about the need to pray. Then they came forward for a time of prayer during which one older man prayed for thirty minutes while the rest of the group fought to stay awake.

It was difficult for me not to become depressed, especially when I knew things did not have to be this way. But I finally gave up trying to convince the people at that church that we needed a small-group system and set out to reach some new people for Christ on my own.

The first thing I did was go downtown and begin to get acquainted with some of the local businessmen. Then I went into a nearby hotel and rented a room, to which I invited these businessmen for an informal Bible study. To my surprise, six of them came! So I continued to rent this room every Wednesday morning, and five of the six men continued to come on a regular basis.

We began to work our way through the Gospel of John, reading it verse by verse and asking three questions as we went along: What does this verse say? What does it mean? How do we use it? By the fourth week, when we had gotten into the third and fourth chapter of John, four of these men made commitments to Christ.

I was overwhelmed! In addition to their receiving Christ, these men began to attend church, bringing their families with them. And do you know what those long-standing, traditional church members said when they saw these new people?

"Who are these people?"

"What are they doing here?"

"Why are they sitting on my pew?"

But eventually their attitude began to change as these new people brought new life into the congregation.

The next thing I did was find some women in the church who I believed truly had a heart for evangelism, and I challenged them to start some new Bible studies in their communities. To my delight, they accepted my challenge! Soon they were reaching women in their neighborhoods with the gospel and then bringing them to church along with their families. The church began to grow as new life emerged around the edges of the traditional church and then infiltrated the church itself. The inner workings of the traditional church hadn't really been disturbed at all, and yet it was beginning to take on healthy new growth. It was an exciting time!

Have you ever seen a cross-section of a large tree, a redwood perhaps? If so, you know the tree grows around the edges and the rings move outward. This is what happened in this traditional church as new life began to enter from the outside edges.

I believe this is the best way to bring new life and vitality to an old church—by creating small groups on the edge or perimeter of the church and then bringing in the new life they create slowly. That way people don't feel as threatened because the elements they are used to and comfortable with are left in place. For example, the Wednesday night prayer meeting can continue but it is now referred to as Group 1. At the same time you free up people to attend a prayer meeting or small-group meeting at another time and/or place, letting them know that they're just as good and faithful a Christian if they attend prayer meeting on Saturday morning as if they attended on Wednesday night. For traditional thinkers, this may be an entirely new concept.

Integrating Small Groups into Any Church

When we first started New Hope Community Church, I had the privilege of creating new paths simply because it was a brand new venture with no traditions to overcome. So I started early with the concept that we would have multiple groups on every day and night of the week. Now years later, that's exactly what we have. That reality grew out of the very first group my wife and I led in our home. Out of that group we trained leaders for the next groups, who in turn trained leaders for the next groups, and we just kept multiplying.

I believe that whether you're in a newer church or an old, established church, the principles I'm going to teach you can be applied for wonderful growth and multiplication of small groups in your church. Creating a sense of participation and ownership in people is the key to successfully using small groups in any church. And a fully integrated system, the system we use at New Hope that incorporates small groups into every aspect of the church, is what I strongly recommend to anyone who wants to see maximum benefit from their small-group ministry. There are five principles that can help assure that a church's small-group ministry is embraced by members and integrated into the church.

1. Make small groups the vision and heart of the senior pastor. In seminar after seminar, people ask me, "Our senior pastor isn't here. Can we do this without him?" I explain to them that it is certainly possible to incorporate small groups into a church without the full support of the senior pastor, but it will never be a fully integrated system and, therefore, will never reach its maximum potential.
2. Make small groups the vision and heart of the church leadership. I intentionally work at seeing that people are nominated for our church board who are already involved in small groups and who believe 100 percent in the vision of small-group ministry at New Hope. People must be united in their pursuit of a vision, and that can only happen when an example is set by leadership.
3. Make small groups a priority in the church's weekly calendar or bulletin. Make sure small group meeting times, places, descriptions, and leaders are advertised prominently in church publications and in announcements.

4. Make small groups a high priority for lay ministry. The highest priority of lay ministry in our church is being involved in small-group ministry. I would not want anyone involved at any level of lay ministry at New Hope who wasn't also involved in and committed to small-group ministry.

5. Make small groups a priority of the pastoral staff. Everyone on our staff either leads a group or assists in leading a group. Our pastoral team is involved in creating new groups, and every pastor on our staff oversees a district of lay pastors who lead small groups. Our pastors know this is what their ministry is all about whether they are over music ministry, children's ministry, or any other ministry.

Keeping Small Groups at a Good Working Number

In addition to making small-group ministry a priority in the church, I believe it is also advisable to keep the size of those small groups at a good working number. Eight to twelve people—ideally ten—are the maximum numbers that I would suggest be in a small group.

In 1940 the Southern Baptists developed what they call the "flake formula." Now this formula has nothing to do with people we often think of as flakes—those who can't be counted on to carry through. The "flake formula" referred to the Southern Baptists' belief that each time a church recruited, trained, and released a new teacher, the church's Sunday school would grow by ten people, which was the average maximum size of a Sunday school class. Many great Sunday schools were built on this principle.

Along with the flake formula is the Jethro principle, taken from Exodus 18. In the Jethro principle, leaders are appointed over groups of one thousand, then one hundred, then fifty, then ten. Researchers also tell us that ten people is about all one person can handle, nurture, and care for; hence, the ten-to-one ratio.

Think of group size in terms of communication interaction. Much verbal and nonverbal communication goes back and forth when you're in a group of people. For instance, if you have two people in a group, each sends out one signal to the other person for two signals. (See figure 1.) But if you have three people, each sends out one signal to each of the other two plus one signal to both (three signals each) for a total of nine signals. As more and more people are added to the group, the communication figure multiplies exponentially. If you have ten people in a group, the figure goes up to 5,110 signals! So you can see that the larger the group becomes, the more difficult it is for the leader to ensure clear and open communication within the group. Besides, most homes won't comfortably accommodate many more than twelve people. Limited parking space around a private home is another built-in factor for establishing group size.

Figure 1   **Signal Counts in Small Groups**

2 people	send out	2 signals
3 people	send out	9 signals
4 people	send out	28 signals
5 people	send out	75 signals
6 people	send out	186 signals
7 people	send out	441 signals
8 people	send out	1,016 signals
9 people	send out	2,295 signals
10 people	send out	5,110 signals

Adapted from Human Scale by Kirkpatrick Sale, in *Prepare Your Church for the Future* by Carl F. George, Revell, 1991.

Managing Group Size by Multiplication

If a group grows beyond a good working size, we never say we are going to divide the group. Instead, we use the word *multiply,* which is a much more positive word. We multiply a group by training an apprentice leader who can go out and start a new group when the existing group becomes too large. To start the new group, we simply invite people in the existing group to go with the new leader to help establish the new group. Invariably, a few people in the group will accept the invitation, and we then have two groups with growth potential. However, we must remember that our focus should never be the number of groups we have, but the new leaders that are growing out of the groups. Those leaders will ultimately create the new groups, not us.

A word of caution: when concerned about group size, it can be very tempting to want to simplify things by assigning people to certain groups. I do not believe this works nearly as well as allowing people to choose which group they want to attend. When you try to "force" people into a group, you will meet with resistance, and they may very well decide not to attend small groups at all.

Organizing Small Groups by Area and Kind

We organize the small groups at New Hope according to the Jethro principle of Exodus 18, which we will discuss further in chapter 5. We use this principle in the following manner:

- One lay pastor cares for one small group of eight to twelve people.
- One lay-pastor leader oversees five lay pastors, or about fifty people.
- One district pastor oversees ten lay-pastor leaders, or about five hundred people.
- One senior pastor oversees all district pastors who, in turn, oversee everyone else.

We have two kinds, or tracks, of districts in the New Hope organizational model. The first track is made up of what we call geographic districts. These districts include general, TLC groups that are organized according to zip codes. At present, we have four geographic districts in our church.

Track two is made up of what we call specialty districts. Our specialty districts include the following:

- *Task district*—includes ushers, parking lot attendants, greeters, and all task-oriented groups.
- *Positive singles district*—includes all young adults, singles, widowed, separated, and formerly married adults.
- *Children's ministries district*—includes children nursery age through sixth grade as well as the staff who serve these ages.
- *New Life Victorious district*—includes people of all ages with compulsive behavior problems, their families, and the staff who serve these ministry groups.
- *Youth district*—includes all young people in junior and senior high as well as the staff who serve them.
- *Young adults district*—includes people from the ages of twenty-four to thirty, whom we call Pacesetters. These people meet together for fellowship, fun, and spiritual growth under the leadership of trained staff.
- *Creative arts district*—includes choirs, orchestra, vocal groups, drama, staging, lighting, and writing.
- *Restoration district*—includes divorce recovery, separation survival, grief recovery, cancer support, reconciliation, Vietnam veterans, and blended families.

Each of our districts, both on track one and track two, has a full-time pastor who works over and with lay pastors, who in turn lead small groups in that district. This is what is known as a "meta-church" model.

How This Structure Evolved at New Hope

Let's take an inside look at the development of the New Hope meta-church model, which now ministers weekly to more than five thousand people in small groups, keeping in mind three key points:

1. Every successful small-group system begins with the first cell group or groups.
2. Small-group ministry has to be built from the ground up.
3. A model group or groups is the way to begin.

Back in the beginning, my wife and I started the first group in our home, and out of that group came leaders who started the next groups and so on. After a few years, we started having regular training sessions. Eventually we established what we now call our "Super Bowl," where we bring people in for their initial training.

About 1984 I almost made a big mistake. At that time we had about thirty or forty groups, and we were adding about four to five hundred members annually. We were growing rapidly, but we also had people going out the back door as quickly as they were coming in the front. Our groups weren't multiplying. So I started looking around the country for someone to come and oversee our small-group ministry.

Well, I looked everywhere, but I just couldn't seem to find the right person. Then one day, in God's perfect plan, I got on a plane and went down to southern California to a conference where Dr. Cho was speaking. (Dr. Cho pastors the largest church in the world, with approximately sixty thousand small groups in their system.) In his talk he explained organizing your church by geographic districts rather than by the traditional departmental model we were using at New Hope at the time—we had a parish-life pastor, an evangelism pastor, a part-time Christian education person, and others.

As I listened to Dr. Cho, the Lord really began to speak to my heart, and I made the decision to go home and reorganize the church, which I did. I put the evangelism pastor at the head of district one and the parish life pastor over district two, but then I discovered I had a problem. I didn't have a pastor for district three.

At the same time I had another problem, one I had been trying unsuccessfully to deal with for quite a while. This problem had to do with my secretary, Betty. Betty had this habit of getting so involved in ministry that she simply wouldn't get my work done. This was a very frustrating situation, to say the least. For example, one day I came into the office and instead of finding Betty at her desk doing the work I'd assigned her to do, I found her in my office praying with someone to receive Christ. Another time I walked in and found her on the phone, praying for healing for the person on the other end of the line. Still another time I found her off counseling someone who had come into the office looking for help with a personal problem.

Well, it took me awhile to put it all together, but I finally figured out what I needed to do—and believe me, it was a big step for me because it ran counter to anything I had ever considered doing before. I took this woman who had never been professionally trained in ministry but who obviously had the gifts necessary for ministry, and I said, "Betty, I want you to take district three." She did (and did a wonderful job of it, I might add), and I hired a new secretary who concentrated solely on getting my work done. It was a wonderful solution!

Now along with the oversight of district three, Betty soon inherited another responsibility. We had a support group at the time that had been started about six months earlier when two recovering alcoholics approached me and said, "We really need to have a ministry for alcoholics. Here's some material about a new-life ministry for alcoholics with Christ as the center. We'd really like to see something like this get started here at New Hope."

I looked over the material and then told them, "Well, I don't know anything about this sort of ministry, but if you guys want to go ahead and get it started, you have my blessing."

So there they were, two recovering alcoholics with some Christ-centered literature, trying to start a ministry for people with alcohol problems. They may not have known much about starting or running a group, but before long there were about fifteen people coming to their group every Monday night. That's when the idea came to me to have Betty oversee the group.

"I'd love to," she responded when I told her my idea. And then she went on to explain that, years earlier, she too had battled with alcoholism. In fact, there had been a history of alcoholism in her family. I hadn't known any of this, but of course God knew, and he knew that Betty's recovery had prepared her for ministry in this special area.

Betty took the group and out of that group she trained more leaders who started new groups, who trained more leaders who started more groups, until I had to create an entire new specialty district called New Life Victorious. Out of this district we minister to people in all kinds of recovery situations. On a recent Monday night, New Life Victorious had more than six hundred people in their groups, all of which were led by people who had grown up out of these recovery ministries, finding wholeness in the process. Now they are equipped and trained to lead others to that same place of healing through the ministry of these small recovery groups.

That's how small groups work. When you really begin to release lay people in small-group ministry, healing happens, and it multiplies to touch countless others. Those two recovering alcoholics didn't know much about starting a small group, but they knew they cared about helping other alcoholics find healing through Jesus Christ. Their caring is what gave them the vision to start the group, not their knowledge. Their knowledge of small-group ministry grew as people came and the group grew. You see, people don't care how much you know until they know how much you care.

I have heard my friend Carl George say, "One of the strengths of a meta-church model is the biblical conviction of the Holy Spirit officially commissioning every believer into ministry for caring for one another."

There is simply no other way to do it effectively.

4

Nuts and Bolts of Small Groups

It is impossible to explain to anyone how small-group ministry works without first explaining exactly what is meant by the term *small group.*

A small group is simply an ongoing relational gathering—a little flock or cell—in which eight to twelve participants model and learn how to care for one another. These groups may be made up of couples, single adults, men only, women only, adults and children, or any combination of these. The discussion within the group must be open and free, with emphasis on biblical application to daily life. Whatever the particular grouping, members learn ways to make their family or single life better.

The leader of each small group must receive careful training and supervision. These leaders grow out of existing groups and then go out and start new groups, out of which new leaders grow who launch another set of new groups.

The net effect of all this lay-driven, small-group ministry is what makes the entire church healthy and successful. The role of the pastoral staff is to effectively train and manage the leadership of the small-group system. When each person involved—pastoral staff, lay leaders, small-group members—understands and operates within this framework, the small-group system will run smoothly and effectively.

Small groups are where people connect with other people, with God, and with the church; they are where heart-to-heart ministry—or "people care"—takes place. As I travel across the country, I hear small groups referred to as cell groups, growth groups, discipleship groups, care groups, and nurture groups. We call our small groups Tender Loving Care or TLC groups because TLC groups are where we gather together in Christ's name and really care for one another. They are where we develop a sense of belonging to and being loved by others. Being a part of a TLC group means being accepted where you are as well as giving acceptance to others in the group. In TLC groups, the circle of love is continually being enlarged to take in one more person.

A few years ago, as a direct result of our small-group ministry, we had the privilege of receiving an award from *Guideposts* magazine. Dr. Norman Vincent Peale came to our church to make the presentation and, along with the mayor of Portland, was a part of the festivities for that event. As I sat talking with the mayor that day he commented, "TLC, TLC—why, that's what everybody needs!" So he went back to his office and issued a proclamation that the very next day in Portland, Oregon, was to be TLC Day—Tender Loving Care Day—in honor of the ministry of small groups at New Hope. We have that proclamation hanging on our wall at the church as a testimony and reminder that *everybody* needs TLC—and small-group ministry is where they'll find it.

Some of the very best friendships my wife, Margi, and I have ever had have been with people in a small group with us. We dearly cherish those friendships, as do so many of our members who have been in small groups for any length of time.

Training Lay People to Facilitate Small Groups

I believe that one of the main reasons small-group ministry is so effective is that trained lay people are doing the majority of the pastoring of the church through shared ministry, shouldering the responsibility along with the pastoral staff who cannot possibly do it alone. By training lay leaders and setting them over small groups, pastoral care is divided into manageable sections.

A lay leader is not necessarily a qualified teacher, but rather a trained facilitator. It isn't that we don't want our leaders to be teachers, but we have discovered two things about teachers: Few people are really qualified to be teachers, and teachers are difficult to reproduce. Facilitators, on the other hand, are simply trained people who can guide discussions and interaction and encourage others to learn and grow together. Facilitators need to have a love for people as well as an ability to guide them. It is much easier to find good facilitators than trained Bible teachers, and they are much easier to duplicate.

Qualifications for Small-Group Leaders

There are five characteristics that we always look for in potential small-group leaders:

1. *Enthusiasm*—My friend Frank Harrington, who pastors the Peach Street Presbyterian Church in Atlanta,

Georgia, says, "One enthusiastic flea can drive a dog nuts!" There is a lot of power in enthusiasm, and it is contagious. We want people leading our groups who are excited about what they're doing because that's what attracts and draws other people to the group.

2. *Clear testimony*—We can't lead people to Christ if we don't know him ourselves. We want our leaders to have a clear testimony for Jesus.

3. *Dedication*—The difference between a champ and a chump is dedication—the dedicated person finds a way to accomplish the vision. We want leaders who are dedicated to living by the Bible, being led by the Holy Spirit, and fulfilling the mission of Christ through our church in our community. We want people who are dedicated to building the small-group system.

4. *Spirit-led life*—Not only do we want our leaders to be filled with the Holy Spirit, we want them to fellowship with the Holy Spirit regularly, flowing with him in ministry. When I read the Book of Acts, I see the Holy Spirit as the center of everything that happens. We want people to know the Holy Spirit, and so we make it a priority to teach about the Holy Spirit.

5. *Time and means*—We need to recognize that the average lay person has about twelve to fourteen hours per week that they can call their own. So if we're going to ask them to give us two or three of those hours in ministry, that's asking a great deal. Some people simply don't have the required time to be lay pastors. We have also had people come in who want to begin training as a lay pastor, but they are having personal problems—an inability to hold down a job or an out-of-control family situation. We sit them down and say, "Before you make a commitment to

get involved in lay ministry, there are some steps you need to take to deal with your personal situation. We will be happy to help you in whatever way we can, but those steps must be taken before you can begin training for lay ministry. Once your personal situation is under control, we'll talk again about the possibility of your becoming a small-group leader." Overlooking these situations leads to disaster. Ultimately, we not only lose the leader, but possibly the people in the leader's group as well.

Meeting Different Needs through Small Groups

At this point, I'd like you to take inventory of all the groups you already have in your church—maybe a men's group, a women's group, ushers, a prayer group, the choir, a drama team, nurturing or care groups, support or recovery groups, youth groups, singles, jail ministry, Bible study groups, seniors, and college/career groups. I think you'll be surprised at how many different ways you already group people in your church. People just seem to gather in groups.

Almost all groups in the church seem to fall into three different categories: nurture or care groups, task groups, and support or recovery groups.

Nurture or care groups. It is important that we discover and emphasize the validity of nurture groups. Ours are called TLC groups, the regular, or more healthy groups in the church. Activities in these groups include application of the Bible, praying, sharing life together, caring for one another, evangelism, encouraging, and discipleship. Every church needs solid and ongoing nurture groups.

Task groups. I wasn't sure what to call these groups until several years ago when I began to read Carl George's manuscript on the meta-church model before it was published. He talked about task groups, so I went to a staff

meeting and wrote on the board, *task groups*. We began to
list the task groups we already had in operation in our
church and, to our surprise, came up with about thirty different groups that we hadn't officially recognized as part
of our small-group system. In fact, we had enough to make
another district of groups that included office staff, janito-
rial staff, ushers, greeters, and so on.

To give you an idea of how a task group works and why
we consider them part of our small-group system, let's look
at the ushers as an example. During the week, if one of the
ushers is sick or in the hospital, another usher will visit
and pray for him. On Sunday, the ushers come in and go
immediately to a room off the main foyer where they have
devotions and pray for one another. Then they go into the
sanctuary to perform their task. We also have a task group
of women who come into the office every Monday morning to count Sunday's offering. One Monday morning I
observed these women standing in a circle around one
woman whose husband was having serious surgery. They
were praying for her and encouraging her. So in addition
to carrying out a task, task groups care for one another.

Support or recovery groups. Support groups are a great
outreach ministry, and there are literally hundreds of different kinds of support groups that can be started in any
church. Many of our support and recovery groups use the
Twelve Steps, and we have just about every type of group
imaginable. What we've found is that if someone has a
need and he or she hears about our support group, it isn't
long before he or she is plugged into that group. In the
group, members learn about Jesus—many for the first time.
They receive the help they need and many are led to Christ.
Before you know it, they're bringing other people with the
same need to the group, and they also receive Christ. It's
one of the easiest, most natural ways to evangelize that
I've ever found.

Let me tell you about a young woman named Marilyn. I was at a training meeting about a year ago when Betty, one of our pastors, introduced Marilyn to me and said, "Marilyn came to me four years ago and told me, 'I really need a group for people who have been sexually abused. I was abused as a child by someone in my own home, and I need a support group.' So I told her, 'Well, we don't have one of those yet, but I've been thinking about starting one, and if you'll be my assistant, I'll lead it.'" So Betty and Marilyn started this group together. Four years later we had five of these groups, and Marilyn was the lay-pastor leader over them. Not only did Marilyn get the help she needed, she expanded the group and helped others become leaders so that many more people could find the help they needed.

Materials for support groups are readily available, especially since support/recovery material has begun to be published in the Christian marketplace. To mention just a couple, Tyndale has a recovery Bible that shows how the Twelve Steps came from the Scriptures. Also a group called Rapha puts out a fine assortment of support/recovery material.

As for support-group leaders, I have personally found that the most effective leaders are those who have come through the program themselves. These people have received help and healing in the group and then feel the call of God to help others who have just come in to the group. It is a proven method of support-group ministry that produces excellent results.

Open versus Closed Groups

Small groups can be classified as either open or closed. Let's take a look at the difference between open and closed groups.

Back in the '60s and '70s when I first began to read about small groups, it seemed that most of the literature I came across had to do with closed groups, commonly called "covenant groups." These groups meet together for a set period of time, say three months, and then stop. But they are not open to bringing anyone new to the group. The problem with having this kind of group in your church is that you are always starting over. It is a bit like climbing a mountain but never getting to the top.

From the first day of small-group ministry in our church, we have believed that small groups need to be open groups—open to people joining at any time. We believe this not only because it is easier to build and maintain this type of system, but because evangelism and outreach are very important to us, and there is very little room for either in a closed-group system. Open groups fulfill the Great Commission of winning the lost to Christ and then discipling them.

We have also found that we become like family in open groups. There is trusting and caring within the group that allows members to quickly accept any newcomers and make them feel welcome. This trust and caring also make people feel free to share what's going on in their lives and to ask for prayer for personal areas without worrying about anyone betraying a confidence. People who have a sense of family and who pray for and care for each other do not use their inside knowledge as a source for gossip.

Open groups are easier to build and maintain because we don't have to start over each time the groups finish their committed time together. We have found that our open groups continue year-round, even in the summertime when church attendance often falls off due to family vacations. Even in the month of August, we still have more than four thousand people attending our small groups each week. When fall comes, we don't have to go through the lengthy, time-consuming process of getting the program up and running again. The groups are already in place and just continue on as always.

The Four Purposes of Small Groups

There are basically four purposes for our small groups, each of which I consider equally important. These purposes are the following:

1. *Evangelism*—I remember being at a training meeting where a white-haired man named John Smith, a retired plumber, came forward. He was weeping tears of joy as he told of three people who had received Christ in their small group that week. John was so excited! He explained that the conversions happened as they discussed one of the questions for that week's lesson, "How does one become a Christian?" One person in the group said, "I really don't know." Two other people chimed in and said they didn't know either. The other members of the group began to share their testimonies of how they had come to Christ. By the end of the evening, they led these three precious people in the sinner's prayer and had the joy of seeing them receive the Lord Jesus Christ. That's how evangelism works in small groups.

2. *Discipleship*—There is no possible way we could begin to teach and disciple all our new converts at New Hope if it weren't for the discipling that takes place within our small-group ministry. In small groups converts begin to learn and grow in the things of Christ, and even have the opportunity for on-the-job ministry training as they grow.

3. *Shepherding*—It is in the small groups that our people-care and heart-to-heart ministry takes place. Lay leaders are doing what our pastoral staff cannot possibly do, giving necessary personal care to thousands of members.

4. *Service*—Small groups provide tremendous opportunities for people to use their gifts in ministry. Great,

untapped resources are discovered and used in small-group ministry.

Although I see all of these purposes as equally important, a healthy small-group system must always see evangelism as its continuing mission. To keep evangelism thriving in small groups, you must continue to push people out of their comfort zones by encouraging them to call on new people, putting the names of new prospects into their hands, and continually keeping the message of evangelism before them.

Leadership within the Small Group

To build and maintain a thriving small-group ministry, I believe it is necessary to have three leadership positions within each nurture or care group: a leader, an assistant leader, and a host/hostess. Filling these positions is essential to prevent leader burnout and build longevity into the groups.

The leader is the facilitator of the group, a lay pastor who has completed lay-pastor training. The assistant leader is the leader's apprentice, a lay pastor in training who assists the leader while preparing to start a new group. The host or hostess takes the pressure off the leader and assistant by providing a home for the group meeting, as well as snacks for any fellowship time. The following are job descriptions for each of these three leadership positions in our small-group system.

Tender Loving Care Group Leader Job Description
(must be a trained lay pastor)
1. Make a phone call and home visit to all prospects, members, and friendship card assignments.
2. Work with the host/hostess to make people comfortable.

3. Talk and pray with the assistant leader and host/hostess before each meeting.
4. Report to the district pastor each month on the progress of the assistant leader.
5. Initiate the conversational prayer.
6. Lead the Bible lesson and discussion.
7. Be responsible for the report of the TLC meeting.

Tender Loving Care Group
Assistant Leader Job Description
(must be a lay-pastor trainee)
1. Make a phone call and home visit to all prospects, members, and friendship card assignments.
2. Open the group meetings.
   a. Introduce guests
   b. Initiate an icebreaker activity: for example, "Today was a good day because..."; "My favorite color is..."; "My favorite time of the day is ..."; "One good thing that's happened since last week is ..."
3. Make announcements as needed.
4. Lead the sharing time.
5. Plan the refreshment schedule.
6. Arrange for babysitting.
7. Lead the lesson and discussion occasionally as requested by the leader.
8. Complete and return the TLC Group Meeting Report sheet.

Tender Loving Care Host or Hostess Job Description
1. Take advantage of the hospitality training that is offered in our church.
2. Provide a comfortable home (or restaurant/business place).
3. Set up refreshments before the meeting time.
4. Arrange chairs in cooperation with the leader.

5. Have extra Bibles and pencils available for those who forget theirs.
6. Show people where to put coats.
7. Set an atmosphere of love and acceptance for everyone—regular attenders and guests.
8. Wait until guests leave before cleaning up and rearranging furniture.

Knowing these job descriptions ahead of time prevents any confusion for those coming in to these positions of leadership. Making sure that all three of these positions are filled prevents burnout among leaders. I remember when my wife and I were leading small groups. We'd been doing it for years, and one Thursday night I came home and Margi said, "Our group's coming in tonight, and I need to have you run the vacuum and help me clean house."

Now, I'd had a long day, and although I knew my wife had also been extremely busy, cleaning house was not what I'd had in mind to do when I came home. For the first time, I found myself dreading our small-group meeting. The situation also gave me some insight into what lay leaders in all churches face—overload! We must set up a system with a fair division of labor so no one person's load is too heavy.

Suggested Order of Service for Small Groups

One of the keys to making small-group ministry work is a suggested order of service for the groups. The following is the one we use for our own TLC groups:

	Suggested Time
1. Opening	2 minutes
Introduction of guests	
Icebreaker activity	
2. Opening prayer	2 minutes

3. Praise	10 minutes
Testimonies	
Singing	
Reports of answered prayer	
Appreciation for each other	
Thanksgiving to God	
4. Conversational prayer	5–10 minutes
5. Bible lesson with	30 minutes
practical application	
6. Intercessory prayer for help	5–10 minutes
in applying the lesson	
7. Closing prayer in	2 minutes
The Lord's Prayer	
Doxology	
Total	60 minutes

Of course we don't necessarily follow this plan rigidly, but these are the elements we want to have in each meeting. We recommend to our leaders that they keep their meetings to one hour. If we don't put some sort of time limit in place, when everyone is having a good time, leaders decide to go another hour—or two! Then pretty soon we have group members coming home from a long day at work thinking, "I'm just too tired to go to the small-group meeting tonight. I'll never make it that long!" We need to look at small-group ministry as "for the long haul." We want people to come back week after week, not just have a good time one week and then not return. So we urge our leaders to stay as close to one hour as possible. After the meeting is adjourned, if people want to stay, then that's up to them, but the rest of the people are free to leave.

The Results of Effective Small Groups

As the small-group system begins to take shape and the leaders learn to conduct the meetings within the suggested time frames and formats, you will notice that the individual groups, although each somewhat different because of the different personalities involved, will begin to take on similar characteristics. We have noticed ten in particular.

1. *They become a close, caring family.* One of the couples who have been with us almost since the beginning—in fact, they found Christ in one of our TLC groups years ago—was coming down the hallway toward me one morning a few months ago. I stopped to visit with them and found out that one of their children had been involved in a hit-and-run accident. He was sentenced to the penitentiary. With tears coming down their cheeks, they said to me, "Pastor, we wouldn't have been able to make it through if it hadn't been for the members of our TLC group standing with us and loving us through it."

I remember another time when a couple in a small group needed $465 so they wouldn't be evicted from their home. I looked around the circle at the people who were there and thought, "I doubt that this group can come up with $25 between them." To my surprise, people began to lay money on the table, and when they were through, the entire amount the couple needed was there for them. Now that's a close, caring family!

2. *They learn to apply the Bible to daily life.* No matter what church you're in, there's always someone who really wants to study the "meat of the Word"—to get into the "deeper things of God." Do you know what we do for these people? We have a Greek class on Sunday morning at 8:30 A.M. They come all excited with their Greek Bibles and their commentaries. The only thing I tell the leader is, "Give them what they want. Let them grind away on their Greek, but please keep them away from me!"

The majority of people don't come to church wanting to study Greek. They are trying to find a way to apply what they're reading in the Bible to their daily lives, trying to make sense of it all so they can get through life one day at a time. And that's what small groups are all about—helping people apply the Bible to the situations they face every day.

3. *They have a place to share and learn from life's testimony.* A man named Jack once said to me, "When you preached on tithing, I said to my wife, 'I'll never do that! He's just after our money. I won't do that for anything!' And then we went to our small group, and they started talking and sharing about tithing—about the blessings they had experienced since they began tithing, about the excitement they felt in their lives at the realization that they were partnering with God through their tithing. Before I knew it, I'd signed up to be one of those tithers! Now I can say that it's one of the greatest things that's ever happened in my life. But, Pastor, I never would have done it through your preaching. I did it through the sharing of the testimonies in our TLC group." People sharing testimony of life is a great way to teach.

4. *They receive effective one-on-one pastoral care.* The nurture or care group is an effective way to give one-on-one pastoral care to an unlimited number of people who otherwise simply wouldn't receive it.

5. *They learn to give each other encouragement and edification.* In small groups, we want to see a great deal of encouragement and edifying of one another. What we find is that when people are edified and built up and learn to encourage others, they go home and begin to use more positive words with their family members, edifying and encouraging them. The atmosphere of the home is transformed to a loving atmosphere where people can grow and become everything God has created them to be. This change begins in a small group where people learn the principles of encouraging and edifying one another.

6. *They are provided with unlimited opportunities for meaningful service.* I want to tell you about one of the first TLC

groups my wife and I had some twenty-plus years ago. One night somebody brought a man to the group who was about 6'10" with a ponytail down his back. His name was Rich. His drug dealer at the International Airport in Portland had led him to Christ. Rich worked for Western Airlines at the time. He didn't have a church home, so he'd just sit around and read his Bible. Well, one night a friend from the airport brought him to our small group, and he fell in love with it and kept coming back. Soon he brought his wife and they joined the church.

One week, when I knew I was going to be gone and we didn't have assistant leaders yet, I looked around the group to choose someone to lead in my absence. They were all relatively new Christians with very little experience in the Bible or in leadership. My eyes landed on Rich. He was obviously the biggest person in the group, so I asked him, "Rich, would you lead the group next week?" He seemed surprised but agreed. I spent a little time helping him prepare for the lesson and then went out of town. When I returned a week later, the group announced that they had enjoyed Rich's leadership so much that they had a better discussion with him than they had when I led the group! Well, rather than feeling threatened, I began to work with Rich, training him to take a group of his own, which he soon did. Before long he was working with others, helping train them for leadership. After a couple of years, he became a member of our pastoral team and served for more than fifteen years in ministry. And it all began in a small group.

7. *They provide non-threatening, friendship evangelism.* A few Sundays ago, I looked up in the baptistry and there were a pastor and a lay pastor baptizing one of the converts that the lay pastor had led to the Lord in a small group. I know of no easier way of evangelizing than bringing people to small-group ministry.

8. *They disciple new converts.* There is also no easier way to disciple new converts than in a small-group setting. In a small group these converts are connected, cared for, and learning and growing in a loving atmosphere.

9. *They provide for personal spiritual growth.* I believe that people grow at least eight times faster when they're in a small group and attending weekly worship/celebration services on Sunday than if they just attended the service itself. I say this from the experience of years of watching people grow as believers. The growth of people in small groups far exceeds that of people who do not get involved in small-group ministry.

10. *They develop strong leadership.* I believe that churches are built by building leaders. And I don't know of a better way to develop leaders than through small-group ministry. Leadership development goes on week after week, month after month, year after year at New Hope through the small-group ministry. We keep building strong lay leaders, and they make the difference in our church's growth and health.

Principles for Effective Small Groups

Finally I want to share with you twenty-one dynamic small-group principles that we have pounded out over the years and that we know really work. When these principles are not put into practice, the quality of the group and what it accomplishes goes down. In other words, these are tested, proven principles.

1. *There are three parts to a successful TLC group:*

- *Sharing a life.* There's nothing like a life-centered testimony to illustrate what is being taught. When people share with a group, they feel more a part of that group.
- *Conversational prayer.* Having a conversation together with God is a quick way to build unity, first by prais-

ing God and then by praying in response to the needs expressed in the group. Start simple with one-sentence prayers on a subject. For example, have one conversational prayer say something like, "Thank you, Jesus, for being here" and then have others join in with short prayers of thanks. The key here is to get good participation. If people hear short prayers they think, *Oh, I can do that*, and they'll join in. But if they hear someone going on and on, they'll feel intimidated and won't join in.

- *Application of the Bible.* People are interested in more than just receiving Bible knowledge. They want to know how to apply Bible truth to make a difference in their lives.

When these three elements are practiced in group meetings over successive weeks, the group will be healthy and will produce healthy, well-balanced Christians. All three of these elements must be used in equal balance for the best results.

2. *Participation is the key to success.* The goal of a leader is not to be the authority or the teacher, but the guide or facilitator of the group.

Take a look at figure 2, "Successful Group Dynamics," on page 72. The top model, where the leader is doing all the talking while the people listen, doesn't work in America because we just like to talk too much! The second model, where the group only responds to the leader's questions, doesn't work any better. The third model is the one we're after. This is good group interaction. We train our leaders to facilitate discussion with active participation of the group.

How people are arranged will make a difference in the way they participate. The best arrangement is a circle with one empty chair. The empty chair represents the person you want to bring into the group and into a relationship with Christ. (See appendix B.)

Don't pressure anyone to pray, read, or speak. The leader should not directly call on anyone. Instead, the leader should help even the most timid members see that they too have something to offer, but without pressuring them. I remember several years ago I was in a group where a woman didn't come back after her first visit. When I called her she said, "Well, I might as well tell you, Pastor, that I'm afraid somebody's going to call on me to read. That just scares me to death!" You see, there are people who are afraid to read, for whatever reason, just as there are people who are afraid to pray. Suppose you are afraid to read and there you are, sitting in a circle, and the leader asks everyone in the group to take a turn reading. That can be a scary experience, and it can keep people from returning to the group.

3. *Begin and close with conversational prayer.* This sets the tone for your small-group gathering. It brings the group immediately into the presence of God, focusing everyone on what the Lord wants to do in the meeting. In closing, we respond to the truth and help each other make application of it in our lives.

4. *Respond lovingly to a need expressed, immediately!* There is something very unloving about letting a person hang when they have just shared a deep, personal concern. Love does not respond tomorrow, but immediately.

How do you teach people to share their needs? James 5:16 says, "Therefore confess your sins to each other and pray for each other so that you may be healed." We need to admit our faults to one another, pray for each other, and become a healing fellowship. We do this by encouraging people to openly share their needs and concerns and then responding immediately.

Teach by example. The leader should open up and share areas of his or her own life and then request prayer. If the leader sets this example, others in the group will follow.

Figure 2
Successful Group Dynamics

1. Discussion promotes action.
   a. Makes them doers (James 1:22)
   b. To apply scriptural principles to life (Matthew 7:24)
2. Discussion develops boldness to witness and explains their faith.
3. Discussion promotes openness.
4. Discussion inspires.
5. Discussion provides reinforcement and clarification.
6. Discussion develops new insight.
7. Discussion develops self-esteem.
8. Discussion provides the leader with clues as to how he should minister.

Not this:

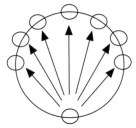

The leader does all the talking and the people all the listening.

Nor this:

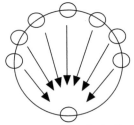

Each group member responds only to the leader's questions.

But this:

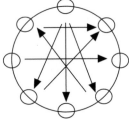

Group members interact with each other, with the leader guiding the discussion.

What are some other ways a group can respond to a member's needs? Have the member sit in a chair in the middle of the circle while the people gather around the "Love Seat," gently lay their hands on the person in the chair, and pray for him or her. God answers prayers of faith and love!

5. *The Bible is our authority and guidebook.* We believe the Word of God contains everything necessary for our salvation and our Christian walk, enabling us to be successful in every area of our lives. On occasion we might allow someone to study from another book. But in the weekly course of small-group ministry, we want all groups to use the curriculum we provide, which teaches applying the Bible in daily living.

6. *Encourage everyone in the group.* Everyone in the group must be made to feel that their ideas and questions are important. Dialogue is what we're after in small groups. However, the group is not a therapy session and the leader is not a psychologist. People with deep emotional problems must be referred to competent counsel.

7. *Don't allow doctrinal discussion that is divisive or argumentative.* Sometimes people would rather discuss doctrinal differences than give attention to what really needs to happen in their own lives. Titus 3:9 says, "But avoid foolish controversies and genealogies and arguments and quarrels about the law, because these are unprofitable and useless." Don't allow discussions on topics that bring division. Instead, focus on studying the Word of God, applying it to daily life, and caring and praying for one another.

8. *Practice mutual edification.* Romans 14:19 tells us, "Let us therefore make every effort to do what leads to peace and to mutual edification." A TLC group should be a team—people helping each other be everything they can be for God. We want to build healthy self-esteem in one another.

9. *Lead in love.* Create an atmosphere of love, acceptance, and forgiveness within the group so that these three attributes are modeled as a way of life. In this environment, people will grow and be healed.

10. *Following-up with members between meetings is essential.* People who are absent need to be called and encouraged. New people must be called in friendship and invited to participate. Regular attenders also need to be called and given words of appreciation.

11. *Bringing new members into the group will keep it alive and growing.* This is why we suggest including an empty chair at each meeting to signify the new person who will soon come to sit in it. New people will help keep a group from becoming ingrown and too comfortable. They bring a new freshness and flavor to the group and keep it vibrant.

12. *Handle problem people away from the group on a one-to-one basis.* This is probably the biggest deterrent to a successful small group. A disturbed person cannot be allowed to become the center of attention in the group. The leader must make it clear that everyone is loved and accepted, but there is "no dumping permitted." If the leader does not enforce this rule, EGRs—Extra Grace Required people—will kill the group. The leader must deal with them lovingly but firmly and quickly. Sometimes these people need to be in a support group for a time until they are healthy enough to participate in a TLC group. Or they may need pastoral counsel from a pastoral team member. They may possibly require professional help at a psychological level. Whatever the problem, the leader must be trained prior to group meetings to handle this type of situation.

13. *Don't allow people to confess anyone's faults but their own.* If this happens, the leader must remind the group of this principle. I'll never forget a group meeting I was in one night. A woman came in with her more-than-slightly-

reluctant husband. In fact, it looked as if she had led him there by the ear. We had no more than started the meeting when this woman announced to the entire group, "Jim is committing adultery." Can you imagine how quiet it got? I looked at Jim, and he was trying to crawl under his chair. So I said to the woman, "We don't confess anyone's sins but our own. Is there anything you'd like to tell us?" It got really quiet again, but then we were able to go on with our meeting. Afterwards at the punch bowl, Jim came over and said, "You know, Pastor, I never saw anyone put my wife in her place before. Thank you!" And do you know what? Jim came back the next week—and the next and the next. That small group became the instrument of healing in that marriage. Jim and his wife each made a recommitment to Christ and began to grow, both in their relationship with God and with each other. But healing can never happen if we allow people to confess the sins of anyone other than themselves.

14. *Don't allow anyone to do all the talking.* If this situation persists, try saying something like, "Thank you for your comments. Now let's hear what someone else has to say," or "Now let's continue with our lesson." We teach our lay pastors to make statements like that to inhibit people from monopolizing all the time and attention.

15. *Make sure the leader is spiritually healthy.* The Holy Spirit will be hindered if the leader is spiritually indifferent or troubled with unconfessed sin. A person who is not free to the workings of the Holy Spirit in his or her own life can hardly be a channel for his working in the group. The Holy Spirit is the great Leader and Teacher, so we really need him in our ministry to be effective.

16. *Make sure the leaders are learning.* We do not expect leaders to know all the answers, but they do need to be learners. The best leaders are good learners. Do you know how freeing it is to lay people to know they don't have to have seven

years of college and seminary to lead small groups? All they have to do is partner with the rest of the group in learning. I can honestly say that the people I have learned the most from are those who are still learning. There is something very creative and attractive about learning together in a group.

17. *Hang loose and maintain a relaxed spirit in the group.* When people are laughing and kidding each other, they're much more relaxed and they receive the truth so much better.

- A leader who exhibits an honesty and openness, who is not afraid to discuss or consider other points of view, and who is free to trust the Holy Spirit to be the teacher is a refreshing example for others in the group to imitate.
- A leader is a tremendous asset when he or she accepts himself or herself as a person of worth and can also reach out to others and make them comfortable with who they are.
- A good leader learns to be shock-proof, not judgmental, harsh, or overly opinionated. When someone in the group says something that's a bit off, a trained leader does not overreact.

18. *A good sense of humor is a valuable asset.* We don't want people to just come in and line up like soldiers on pews. We want them to come in, sit around the circle, have conversation, relax their bodies, relax the tensions of life, rest their spirits, renew their hearts, and enjoy one another. According to Proverbs 17:22, "a cheerful heart is good medicine"—laughter releases tension, renews our hearts, and reorients our life perspective.

19. *When you have a need in your own life, ask your group for help.* We never outgrow our need for help from other Christians. The best leaders are those who keep admitting that they need the help of others. Sit in the "Love Seat" in the middle of the room and let the group members pray for you. I guarantee you, soon they'll all want to sit in that chair and be prayed for.

20. *When you have problems or need help, quickly go to your pastor or leader and ask for it.* At our church, we accept each other where we are and work hard to help each other be overcomers, successful in life and in ministry.

21. *Remember, it is Christ who does the leading, not us.* A good leader is a good follower of Christ—no more, no less.

Care for People Outside of Small Groups

With all these plans and pointers I've shared, I wish I could tell you that everyone at New Hope is now involved in small groups. Most are, but there are still some who are not, although we never give up trying to get them involved. In the meantime, however, we've devised a tele-care system that monitors and ministers to those outside the small-group ministry system. It is a large and very effective system comprised of volunteers who come to the church offices at various times throughout the week and call all those who are not actively involved in small groups. If you are interested in establishing a tele-care system in your own church, just write to us at New Hope and request the tele-care package.

5

Lay Leaders
Share the Ministry

There's a story about a man who went to the local zoo looking for a job. The personnel manager told him, "Well, we do have one job opening. I don't know if you'll want it though. You see, our gorilla died and we need somebody to put on the gorilla suit and get in the cage and beat his chest and act like a gorilla."

"No problem," the man answered. "In fact, it sounds like fun!"

So the man came in to work the next day, put on the gorilla suit, got in the cage, and beat on his chest. And the people around the cage started cheering. The more they cheered, the more excited he became. Pretty soon he climbed up on the swing and started swinging back and forth, back and forth, higher and higher into the air, until he finally was so high he broke right through his cage into the lion's cage next door. The next thing he knew he was lying face down in the lion's cage with the lion's big paw on the back of his neck.

"Help! Help!" he screamed. "Somebody get me out of here! I'm not really a gorilla."

The lion's paw pressed tighter against his neck. "If you don't shut up," a voice behind him whispered, "we're all gonna lose our jobs!"

Right about now, there's bound to be some pastors reading this book thinking, "Galloway, if you don't shut up about these small groups and lay pastors, we're all going to lose our jobs!" But the truth is, the kinds of things I'm sharing with you will only help to make you look good. In fact, I like to say to my lay pastors, "You know, you people make me look so good as a pastor! I get a lot of credit for all the ministry that goes on around here when it's really all of you out there doing the work. I thank you for it, and I bless you, in Jesus' name. Keep up the good work!"

A Closer Look at Lay Pastors

In the last chapter, I touched a bit on the role of lay leaders within the group. But now I would like to zero in on the lay pastors themselves. What is a lay pastor? What exactly does a lay pastor do? And why do we call them lay pastors?

Actually, you can call lay pastors anything you choose, but we call them lay pastors simply because we feel the title best describes what they do. They are people from the laity (nonclergy) of the church who help the pastoral team pastor the people.

I personally love the title pastor. I suppose you could refer to me as "Dr. Galloway" or "Reverend Galloway" or "Mr. Galloway," but I prefer the title "Pastor Galloway." It sounds warm and caring, and that's what I want to be. It is also the way I see our lay leaders, so I want to give to them the title I value most. And because they work at other jobs and don't get paid for working in ministry like I or the other pastors on my staff do, we add the word "lay" to their title. We are blessed to have each and every one of them. A lay pastor is someone who has answered a call from God to do the work of ministry. At New Hope Community Church, our lay pastors are given permission to do all the ministry activities our staff pastors are paid to do, with a few exceptions. Our paid staff preaches and administers the sacraments, although we do allow our lay pastors to serve communion from time to time and even participate in the baptism of new converts who come to know Jesus through small-group ministry. The only other limit on our lay pastors is their own time schedule.

Some lay pastors, because of their financial independence, are able to work full-time in ministry. Others who work at secular jobs to support themselves and their families can give only the minimum of three hours per week. We adjust the lay-pastor ministry so that it fits the amount of time each person has to give, recognizing that people must support themselves and their families, not only physically but emotionally and spiritually. There is no way we could afford to hire people for the thousands of hours of ministry carried on each week by our dedicated and trained lay pastors.

Actually, over the years the difference between ordained clergy, as those of us on paid pastoral staff are often called, and lay people in ministry has almost disappeared. Both those who get paid and those who volunteer are just people ministering to people. We have become a team, and we see clergy and laity in partnership together. I believe that's the way it's supposed to be.

Biblical Qualifications for Lay Pastors

Did you know that you can read about the selection of the first seven lay pastors in the church (including

Stephen, who was later martyred) in Acts 6? They were selected for the same reason Moses instituted the Jethro principle—the needs of the people simply weren't being met. Let's look in Acts 6 for the five qualifications listed there for lay pastors:

1. Must be full of the Holy Spirit—vv. 3, 5
2. Must be full of wisdom—v. 3
3. Must be full of faith—v. 5
4. Must be full of grace—v. 8
5. Must be full of power—v. 8

These seven men were chosen because the apostles could no longer handle the day-to-day needs of the people. They needed help, so they chose godly men to oversee these needs and they refocused their attention on prayer and spreading the gospel—what Jesus had called them to do. These seven men grew to become leaders themselves. This would not have happened if the apostles had not been willing to let go of this part of the ministry.

You see, that's how God works. First he gives you a vision, and that vision is so great and wonderful that there is no possible way you can accomplish it by yourself. God has never given me, as the leader of this church, a vision for ministry that I could do alone. It has always required recruiting other people to help me see that vision through. That is why I say that recruitment is need-driven.

A pastor once said to me, "If getting larger means more work, I don't want to grow because I'm working right at the edge of burnout now."

I told him, "What I want to teach you is that you can grow larger and actually have more time to yourself if you'll really learn how to partner with lay people in ministry."

The Roles of Lay Pastors

The lay pastors in our church actually help fulfill four different roles:

1. *Evangelist*—going out into their communities to proclaim the gospel (see Matt. 28:18–20)
2. *Connector*—standing with one arm out to the people and one to God (see 2 Cor. 5:19–20)
3. *Shepherd*—caring for the people in heart-to-heart ministry (see John 21:15–17)
4. *Servant*—partnering with pastoral staff as servant-leaders (see Matt. 20:25–28)

I am constantly reminding both the pastors on our pastoral team and our lay pastors that being servants *is* our ministry. I tell them that we can only find ourselves as we lose ourselves in the cause of Christ. Our lay pastors are the finest role models of that truth that I have ever seen anywhere.

We will go into more detail about the lay pastor role in small-group ministry in the next chapter. But first I want to take a moment to expand our previous discussion of the Jethro principle.

The Jethro Principle Expanded

Basically, the Jethro principle is a way to help you accomplish more in less time. It is named after the father-in-law of Moses who first presented this idea to him in Exodus 18:13–27. Jethro had been observing Moses and readily recognized that the people-care among the Israelites was limited because it was given by one man—Moses. As I discussed in chapter 3, one person can effectively care for only a small number of people—usually eight to twelve—a good rule of thumb for us to remember as we attempt to care for the people in our congregations.

By studying the Jethro principle, we can learn practical ideas that can be applied in our own lives. Let's look at three examples of problems that were not only common in Moses' time but are common in ours as well—problems that can be solved and/or prevented by applying the Jethro principle: burnout, dissatisfaction, and an unhealthy reliance on leaders.

Burnout. As a young pastor, I used to think that the more hours I worked, the better pastor I was. I have since discovered that this is not necessarily true. A good pastor (or leader of any kind) is not one who does the work of ten people, but rather one who gets ten other people to do the work of ten people. That is what Jethro convinced Moses to do, and it is a great example for us today.

Dissatisfaction. In every marriage, every organization, and every church, there is a level of satisfaction and a level of dissatisfaction. Years ago I mistakenly believed that I could make everyone happy. Well, I soon learned the truth—that I can't even make one other person happy! It was quite a revelation.

I suppose I first began to realize this during my first pastorate. It was in a denomination that had pastoral votes. I'll never forget the first no vote I received. I think maybe twenty people voted yes and one voted no, but I was really hurt by that one no. I thought that if I was going to be a good pastor, I was supposed to make everyone happy. Now, of course, I know better.

The point of this is, when people are not using their spiritual gifts, they're not going to be happy. But the more you help them take ownership of a ministry, the higher their satisfaction level will be. We have over five hundred lay pastors, and if you'd come and talk to one or all of them, you would find that they are very excited leaders. They love what they're doing, and that satisfaction level encompasses all of our church life. Take time to build the satisfaction level of your leadership, and their excitement will spill over into your entire congregation.

Unhealthy reliance on leaders. A few months ago I had an appointment for lunch with one of my pastor friends. I arrived early and sat outside his office to wait for him. We were supposed to meet at 11:30, but I noticed all these other people lined up outside his office waiting to see him, too. After an hour, I was still out there, waiting, as I watched people go in and out of his office. So I decided to walk down the hall and check on his associate pastor. I got to his office and looked through his open door. He was sitting at his desk watching a ball game and drinking a soda.

When the pastor was finally free, we went to lunch and I asked him, "What's your associate pastor supposed to do?"

He smiled and answered, "I'm still trying to figure that out."

Here was a man who thought he had to do all the ministry himself, while a perfectly capable associate sat down the hall watching a ball game! He had created a very unhealthy dependence on himself as leader. The people came to him for everything, and he was wearing himself out—which is exactly what Moses was doing when Jethro suggested he divide the responsibilities of ministry among appointed lay leaders. In fact, the one word that describes what Jethro told Moses to do is *decentralize*, a fancy word for shared ministry. This means you quit trying to do it all yourself and get the ministry down to the grass roots, down to the people where it belongs. The fact that Moses took his father-in-law's advice and put the principle into practice shows that Moses was secure enough to listen to the advice of others. Are we as secure?

Actually, if we look at the eighteenth chapter of Exodus, we will see that Jethro advised Moses to do six things:

1. *Select.* v. 21—Choose capable men.
2. *Train.* v. 20—Teach them the laws and how to live.
3. *Organize.* v. 21—Organize them.
4. *Set up a chain of command.* v. 22—Jethro told Moses to let the other judges take care of the easier problems and bring only the most difficult to him.
5. *Delegate.* v. 22—My friend and fellow pastor David Durey, who sometimes works with me on seminars, gave me a book on leadership because he knows that I like to read that kind of thing (*Increasing Your Leadership Confidence,* by Bobb Biehl). In it I discovered the most wonderful thought: If you can find someone who can do something 80 percent as well as you can, delegate it! This is not what we normally do, is it? We don't want to delegate anything to anyone who can't do it 100 percent as well as we can! But how did I learn to preach a sermon? By others waiting until I was every bit as good as they were to give me a chance? Of course not! A pastor let me preach a sermon in his church when I was seventeen years of age, and that's how I learned. We need to do the same thing if we are ever going to release people for ministry. People learn ministry by doing ministry, and it's up to us as leaders to give them the opportunity to learn it.
6. *Balance his life.* By doing the five points listed above, Moses balanced his life. He now had time for God, for his family, and for himself.

What did Moses encourage people to do that is the same thing we have to encourage people to do today? He urged them to take ownership. Whenever you encourage people to take ownership of a particular ministry, that ministry is going to begin to thrive. As a result of instituting the Jethro principle, Moses became healthier and better able to do his own job. In addition, the new leaders were happy and growing because they were using their spiritual gifts. And the people experienced a new level of satisfaction as their needs were met more efficiently.

There are four reasons why pastors do not put the Jethro principle into practice.

1. *Ignorance.*
2. *Lack of information.*
3. *Insecurities*—This is the biggest problem that keeps pastors from really sharing the ministry. Let's confess, we all have our own insecurities. I have mine; you have yours. One of my prayers for you is that you will grow in God's love and become so secure in that love that you really can begin to free others in ministry and rejoice in their success. Remember that as others succeed in ministry, you also become a more successful pastor or leader. One of our greatest callings is to make other people successful in ministry.
4. *Traditions*—How do you change traditions? Very slooooowly. Just remember—be patient. It really can be done.

We are taught in Ephesians 4:11–13 that the proper relationship between clergy and laity is a partnership in ministry. The clergy are the coaches, modeling ministry while they teach others. The laity are the team members, learning ministry through on-the-job training. Leadership development is essential to all church growth. Only what we share in ministry will multiply. Like loaves and fishes, the more we give away, the more miracles are multiplied in our ministries.

6

Making Small-Group Leaders Effective

The fact that you have read this far in this book probably means that you want to see a successful small-group system operating in your church, a system that is multiplying, where people are coming to Christ and being discipled, and where people are receiving personal pastoral care. If this is your desire, then I believe the following concepts pertaining to lay leaders will be the keys to unlocking your door to a successful small-group system. These are the seven key concepts: requirements, advancement, training, supervision, accountability, recruiting, and the training event.

Requirements for Lay Leaders

It is vital that people know exactly what is expected of them before they commit to being a lay pastor. So what exactly is required of a lay pastor at New Hope? There are twelve basic requirements.

1. To be consistent and committed in living the Christian lifestyle with a daily commitment to prayer as a top priority.
2. To catch the vision of the church and be loyal to its leadership, committed to accomplishing the great things God has called us to do.
3. To be dependable and accountable to those placed in leadership over you.
4. To be led and controlled by the Holy Spirit—something I can't emphasize enough! The Holy Spirit is our guide, our teacher, our motivator. He must be at the center of everything we do.
5. To be a regular participant in a small group, either by leading a group or assisting in the leadership of that group.
6. To be committed to attending a weekly lay-pastors training meeting. We probably have at least six or seven different times now when people come for training. When we were a small church, we just had one time, which I led. The point is, the training must be at the convenience of those who are being trained. For example, many lay pastors in our westside district, which is the farthest away from our church, come in for the training session held during our first Sunday morning celebration service. Then after training they can attend the second service before driving back home. This saves them an extra trip and works out well for them. So find a time that's convenient for those you are training.
7. To wear the lay-pastor badge each Sunday. All of our lay pastors have badges with their names on them so they can be easily identified. The badges enable our lay pastors to easily connect with people in need. Our lay pastors are trained to be sensitive to the needs people have and to respond to those needs.

The badges also give high visibility to the lay-pastor ministry.

8. To come to the Garden of Prayer and pray for those who come forward. In every service, we have a Garden of Prayer at the front of the church where people with needs can come and pray. Our lay pastors come and lay hands on the people who are kneeling while the pastor prays. This is a tremendously effective way to touch people and to establish a connection between them and the lay pastors.

   I recently met a man who had come to our church for the very first time. During the Garden of Prayer time, he came forward and knelt down. When he rose up after prayer, he said, "I don't know who that angel was who touched me, but I felt it while I was praying." When I explained that it was one of our lay pastors, he said it meant a great deal to him that someone would come and gently touch him and pray for him. The lay pastors' involvement in the Garden of Prayer is a very important part of that time.

9. To work faithfully and diligently each week doing the work God has called each one to do.

10. To be a member of our church, complete the special lay-pastor training including passing a written exam, and then be selected by the pastoral staff. We believe membership is important because when a person becomes a member, he or she has made a commitment. Becoming a lay pastor is then moving into another level of commitment.

   We've actually had people come to our church and say they wanted to be lay pastors, go through the training, and then tell us they are not members of the church. We explain to them that they must first go to our membership class, which is an introduction to New Hope, because we want them to be well informed about the church before they begin trying to minister to others. Commitment is a priority.

11. To be faithful in tithing and giving time. Why do we require tithing? Because one of the main ways we teach tithing is through our lay-pastor-driven small-group ministry. People can't teach what they don't know or practice.

12. To maintain a solid family life. Approximately 35 percent of our congregation are single people, so when we say solid family life, we mean that all lay pastors should maintain healthy relationships with those who are closest to them, including their families.

Now you may or may not agree with the list of requirements we have here at New Hope. Feel free to take what you can use—add to it, cut it down, make it your own. But it is essential that you give to your leaders a list of exactly what is required of them before they agree to commit to leadership positions.

Advancement for Lay Leaders

One of the weaknesses I see in many churches is that there is no way for lay people to advance in ministry. Growing and advancing in ministry is essential to successful small-group ministry. This is why we give our leaders opportunity to advance by having three different levels in our lay-pastor ministry.

- Level one—trainee, or assistant lay pastor
- Level two—lay pastor
- Level three—lay-pastor leader

Everyone who comes into our lay-pastor ministry begins at level one as a trainee and begins to serve at that level. After ninety days of faithful service, they become lay pastors.

Training Lay Leaders

How do we train leaders? Thoroughly! We tell existing leaders looking for potential lay pastors, "You supply the person, we'll supply the training."

We incorporate four different types of training into our very thorough training program for lay leaders. These four types of training complement one another and build a solid, ongoing training program for lay people at all three levels.

1. *Initial training*—If someone wishes to become a lay pastor, he or she comes to the initial training time, which is called "Super Bowl." This training time includes sessions on Thursday night, Friday night, and all day Saturday.
2. *Weekly training*—Regardless of their level, all lay leaders must attend weekly training sessions. This attendance is vital to maintaining an attitude that is open to learning and growing. At these weekly sessions, lay pastors receive their lessons, turn in reports, and have a time of sharing together.
3. *On-the-job training*—People learn by doing. On-the-job training is a very effective means of training and equipping lay leaders.
4. *Continual training*—We often hold seminars for our lay leaders on how to better minister to the people God brings to them.

How does the pastoral staff fit into all of this? We train ourselves so we can better train others. I congratulate you on reading this book on lay-pastor-driven small-group ministry because you're training yourself so you can better train others. That excites me! I can see a wave going out, on and on, to thousands and thousands of people in small-group ministry.

Carl George sent his people across the country asking lay people, "What do you see as your needs for training in lay ministry?" The results are in the following table.

Fifty Topics for In-Service and On-the-Job Training

Here are recommended topics taken from Carl George's research (see *Prepare Your Church for the Future*, pp. 142–43) of many churches and the needs that lay pastors have expressed.

1. Listening
2. Responding
3. Challenging
4. Confronting
5. Evangelism
6. Vision/strategy
7. Leadership
8. Recruitment
9. Follow-up
10. Nurturing
11. Communicating the whole picture
12. Administration
13. Problem handling
14. How to run a meeting
15. How to facilitate sharing
16. Counseling
17. Discernment
18. Credibility/example
19. Spiritual knowledge
20. Bible knowledge (lesson preparation)
21. How to reproduce apprentices
22. How to divide/birth a group
23. How to make contacts with new prospects
24. How to welcome newcomers
25. Leading worship and music
26. Identifying spiritual gifts

27. How to link up with outreach projects
28. When to ask for assistance
29. How to pray for healing
30. Managing disruptions
31. Handling child care
32. Deliverance
33. Recognizing abuse
34. Holistic health
35. Time management
36. Loyalty/teamwork
37. Affirmation
38. Attitudes
39. Conflict management
40. Personal disciplines
41. How to teach about prayer
42. How to listen to God in prayer
43. Referrals
44. Legal implications
45. Confidentiality
46. How to share ministry as a team
47. Overcoming shyness
48. Stewardship/budgeting
49. Pastor/shepherd skills
50. One-on-one discipling skills

As you can see, there are a number of different subjects that can be taught during lay-pastor training times.

Supervision of Lay Leaders

We discussed supervision to some degree in chapter 1, but I want to expand on it now. What do we look for in supervision of groups?

In our experience, we have found that our groups are so much more effective when we conduct regular, systematic supervision. When we neglect to supervise a group, the quality of the group deteriorates. All of the pastors on our pastoral staff are involved in supervising small groups. Our lay-pastor leaders assist the pastors in this supervision. A pastor or lay-pastor leader visits and observes a group every six to eight weeks. We check for seven things when supervising small groups:

1. Check the organization to see that the three leadership positions are filled—leader, assistant leader, and host/hostess.
2. Check the prospect list to see if it's up to date. We must keep building prospect lists because they are the first step to outreach through small-group ministry.
3. Check the progress on the small group's goal of adding one family every six months. Think how exciting the fulfillment of that goal is! If you have ten groups, with 2.8 people to a family, and these groups bring a family to Christ every six months, that's almost sixty new converts yearly through your ten groups. Do you see the tremendous growth potential in small-group ministry?
4. Have the leader name his or her hot prospects. On the list of ten people, who are the ones the leader is really going to go after this week to bring into the group?
5. Have the leader name any potential lay pastors. Who in the group has a good potential for being the next apprentice? Have the leader begin talking to that person about attending the next major training event.
6. Observe the use of the twenty-one principles for successful small-group ministry listed in chapter 4.

7. Give counsel for how to deal with any EGRs—Extra Grace Required people—who may be causing difficulty in the group.

Most of all, when we visit the groups for supervision, we want to be encouragers. We have found that the more we encourage our leaders, the more they thrive. Pray with them and for them. Boost them! Sometimes a phone call at just the right moment can make all the difference with a discouraged leader. That word of encouragement can get them up on top again, instead of being down at the bottom feeling defeated.

Accountability of Lay Leaders

Accountability is missing in so many small-group systems, and yet it is absolutely vital for healthy small groups. Here are some steps that we have found helpful in establishing accountability in the small-group system:

Insist that lay leaders make the commitment to be involved in ministry and to come to training every week. At the end of their initial training time, lay pastors in training fill out a "Lay Pastor Commitment Sheet."

Lay Pastor Commitment Sheet

I. I _____, before my Lord Jesus, commit myself to serve him and his church and live in ministry to each other and mission to the world by being a lay pastor.

        Address/Zip Code _____

        Phone Number(s) _____

II. If chosen to be a lay pastor at_____ Church, I commit myself to:

        Pray daily for an extended time.

        Live by the Bible.

        Be a scriptural tither.

        Be faithful and loyal to the church and its leadership.

        Allow the Holy Spirit to control my life.

Attend a regular weekly lay-pastor training
meeting.

III. Catching the vision to serve as a lay pastor for this year I plan to:

Lead a TLC group
Assist in leading a TLC group

Figure 3

L.P.Trainee ☐
Lay Pastor ☒
Senior L.P. ☐

Weekly Ministry Report

Name _Ralph Miller_

Date _Oct. 8, 1994_
District No. _3_

Prayed each day _Yes_	E - Evangelism	L - Letter or Note
Tithed _Yes_	D - Discipled	HO - Hospital
Read my Bible _Yes_	P - Prayer	C - Counseling
Shared Christ's love _Yes_	TLC	HE - Helps
Attended TLC _Yes_	PH - Phone	S - Social
TLC Number _3-16_	PV - Personal Visit	

Write names of people you ministered to this week and how, using the code

CODE	NAME	CODE	NAME
PH	Harpel Sutcliffe	PH	Gary and Dawn Martin
HE - P	Sam Bollet	PV	Matt and Betty Allen
PV - C	John Kruger	PV	Chris and Barb Sanders
PV	Millie Turner	PV	Holly Kartner
PV	Jack and Jill Fondrey	PH	Chip Halten
TLC	"	S	Company picnic - 30
D	Tony Kearns	S	Munnicks and Pondas - 7
L	Eric Taylor		
L	Nicole Harris		
L	Jon Lawrence		
E	Robert Price		
		Total Contacts	69

It is important to hold lay leaders accountable for what they have committed to do. They should fill out weekly report sheets. See samples in figures 3, 4, and 5.

You are welcome to use these commitment and report sheets in any way you like. Change them, adapt them, or do whatever is necessary to make them fit your church.

Figure 3 (continued)

Please use back for: 1) Praise Reports 2) Problem areas 3) Information pastoral staff needs to know about yourself and people you are working with 4) Answered prayers.

I've only been a Lay Pastor for six months and already I have seen the fruit the Lord has given—evidence that this is the ministry for me. Praise the Lord—and thank you New Hope Family!

Have you spent quality time with your family this week? _____
Do you need to talk with your District Pastor? _____

My goals as a lay pastor for	1986	Progress toward my goals this week:
Leading someone to Christ	6/yr.	3 this year
Discipling others	1/week	2 this week
Bringing someone to my TLC	10/yr.	6 this year
Finding new prospects	20/yr.	4 new this week
Making personal contacts	25	+44 this week (PTL!)
Helping others	1/week	2 this week
Leading someone to membership	4/year	2 this year

We require that every lay leader fill out a report of his or her personal ministry for the week. Either the leader or the assistant also fills out a separate report on the small-group meeting each week and brings it in. Then each pastor reads those reports for his district and makes a composite report. On Wednesday the pastors bring their own personal ministry report to my secretary along with the district report.

Figure 4

Lay Pastor Leader Weekly Ministry Report	Date _____ District No. _____

Name _____ TLC's Supervised _____

Prayed each day	_____	E - Evangelism	L - Letter or Note
Tithed	_____	D - Discipled	HO - Hospital
Read my Bible	_____	P - Prayer	C - Counseling
Shared Christ's love	_____	TLC	HE - Helps
Attended TLC	_____	PH - Phone	S - Social
TLC Number	_____	PV - Personal Visit	

Write names of people you ministered to this week and how, using the code

CODE	NAME	CODE	NAME
			Total Contacts [ ]

Then we compile all the district reports and pass out the "Pastors Report Sheet" in our Friday staff meeting (see figure 6).

We closely watch how many lay pastors come to training, because people who don't come to training tend to drop out of ministry. Of course, on any given week someone will be unable to attend for some reason, but if that

Figure 4 (continued)

Names of lay pastors you supervise	Brief report of your contact with them this week

Have you spent quality time with your family this week? _____
Do you need to talk with your district pastor? _____

My Goals as a Lay-Pastor Leader _____	Progress toward my goals this week:
Leading someone to Christ _____	_____
Discipling others _____	_____
Bringing someone to my TLC _____	_____
Finding new prospects _____	_____
Making personal contacts _____	_____
Helping others _____	_____
Leading someone to membership _____	_____
_____ _____	_____
_____ _____	_____
_____ _____	_____
_____ _____	_____
_____ _____	_____

person is not there the following week or the next, we talk to them, find out what the problem is, and discover how we can help. We encourage and pray for each of them and make sure that they follow through on their commitment to attend training regularly.

Figure 5

TLC No. _3-16_   **Weekly TLC Report**   Meeting Date _Oct 8, 1994_
Leader _Ralph Miller_   District No. _3_
Ass't Leader _Pat - Terry_   Host/Hostess _Maylean_

Names of Group Attendants

1. Helen Kruger   M
2. John Kruger   NC
3. Jill Fondrey   M
4. Don Hannum   V
5. Barbi Hannum   V
6. Ruth Paulan   M
7. Howard Beech   R
8. Ralph Miller   L
9. Pat Miller   AL
10. Terry Braum   AL
11. Maylean Barber   H

First-time visitors _2_
Return visitors _9_
& reg. attenders _/_
Total attendance _11_

Mark "V" for visitor; "RV" for return visitor; "R" for regular attender;
"M" for member, New Hope; "H" for host; "NC" for new Christian;
"L" for leader; "AL" for assistant leader.

Starting time for your study _1:30 pm_ What time did study start? _1:35 pm_
What was approximate length of study? _1 hour and 15 minutes_
Was conversation prayer used? _yes_ How long spent in prayer? _15 min._
In Bible Application? _45 min._ in sharing? _____
On a scale of 1 to 10, rate the quality of your group experience this week. Be honest!
1 2 3 4 5 6 7 8 9 (10)
If less than 5—why? _____
Do you need to have a talk with your District Pastor? _no_

Recruiting Lay Leaders

At New Hope, we believe in recruiting. We teach recruiting. We preach recruiting. We model recruiting.

I was at a breakfast in Seoul, Korea, one morning with Dr. Cho and six other pastors. We were sitting around the table

Figure 5 (continued)

Please use back for: 1) Praise Reports 2) Problem areas 3) Information pastoral staff needs to know about yourself and the people you are working with 4) Answered prayers.

God has really answered prayer in John's life and he is such an encouragement to our whole group! Helen has been a faithful Christian and now we get to be part of the harvest time. He's going to need a lot of prayer but we have a great TLC when it comes to praying for each other.

We'll be with John and Helen on Sunday and we'll introduce them to you.

Our TLC Goals for: 1994		This Week	Last Week	Increase/ Decrease	Year to Date
Conversions	Year 4	-	-	-	2
Prospects	Week 25	30	28	+2	
Attendance	Week 10	11	9	+2	
New visitors	Week 1	2	-	+1	
Joined church	Year 4	-	1	+1	2

Figure 6

Pastor's Report for November 20, 1994

District # and Pastoral Leader	TLC Attendance	New Visitors	# of TLC Groups On-Line	# of TLC Groups Meeting This Week	Total # of Lay Pastors	% of Lay Pastors in Training	Total Contacts in District	# of Groups Supervised	# of Lay Pastors Worked With	Total # Contacts by You	Focus 50-5-15 Yes or No
#1 Judy Kennedy	173	4	40	28	52	83	3702	6	16	511	yes
#2 Dennis Deardorff	228	2	49	26	52	75	2436	8	18	231	yes
#3 Wendell Morton	155	6	38	21	43	58	1900	7	12	702	no
#4 David Durey	175	4	30	20	51	62	1189		20	162	yes
#20 Jerry Schmidt	215	4	42	34	26	96	1895	22	24		
#21 Rick Martinez	816	18	44	44	35	80	2059	23	16	1370	
#22 Clara Olson	1612	21	107	77	75	61	3920	40		1003	
#23 Betty Jacques	696	19	62	49	74	75	1754	9	17	400	
#24 Bob Kavanaugh (Jr)	179	20	11	11			1162	11	4		
#25 Bob Kavanaugh (Sr)	235	14	11	11	28	65		11	2	1162	
#27 Wes Walterman	365		1	19	28			19	28	354	
#28 Jeff Hoover	247	10	29	23	17	91	1085	4	3	275	
#29 Jeff Hoover	85	2	6	2	10	60	253	2	2		
#30 George Matteson	292	7	18	16	26	70	601	3	3	157	
#55 Floyd Schwanz	120	4	20	12	10	70	864	2	21	409	
Totals	5593	135	508	393	527	73	22,820	167	186	6736	

chatting when one of the pastors asked, "Dr. Cho, where do you get leaders for your sixty thousand small groups?"

Without even stopping to think, Dr. Cho answered, "We get them from our new Christians."

Now I relaxed because, essentially, we do the same thing. Of course, I don't mean to imply that we take brand new Christians and throw them into leadership. But we do work with new converts to bring them into some level of leadership. We start with small areas of responsibility first, then move them into greater areas as they grow and mature. We tap into their newfound enthusiasm right away rather than leaving them on the sidelines where their enthusiasm and joy lose their sparkle. Recruit and develop them in ministry right away!

Everyone in leadership at New Hope is involved in recruiting—the pastoral staff as well as the lay pastors. One of our lay pastors once wrote these words: "It sometimes amazes me to realize that I'm allowed to lead a small group. I know what I'm doing out there—I'm overtly leading a small group; covertly, I'm training future lay pastors. I know that, the staff at New Hope knows that, but the people who comprise my small group don't have a clue that I'm seeking out new people to take my place. What a wonderful opportunity!"

The key place for recruiting is in our small groups. I also recruit in sermons every time I get the chance. For example, if I have an illustration about a lay pastor and a small group, I'll put that right in the heart of the sermon. I accomplish two things that way—I illustrate my point and I also advertise the joy and opportunity for ministry available to lay pastors. We recruit through all the different ministries of our church, although I've discovered some of the best recruiting is done one on one.

Recently I was recruited myself—to serve on the Boy Scout Committee of greater Portland. I knew ahead of time that the man who was going to meet me for breakfast was going to try to recruit me, and I had already decided I was not going to be recruited. I was far too busy to take on another responsibility. But as I sat down for breakfast, here came this man with two of his friends. All three of them were CEOs with large companies, and they sat there in front of me, each recruiting me *one on one* until I found myself accepting the position. Had they not taken the time to recruit me one on one, I never would have said yes to their offer.

The reason most people don't volunteer is because no one asks them personally. Mrs. Marshall Fields of Chicago once gave one million dollars to the University of Chicago, but she gave not one dime to her denominational school. When asked why, she replied, "No one from my denominational school asked me, but the University of Chicago did."

The Bible tells us that we do not have because we do not ask (see James 4:2). The principle is this: The most talented people will not respond to general or bulletin announcements. They will respond only when you recruit them one on one. So write down their names, pray over them, and work with them individually. Recruit one on one.

The Training Event

Super Bowl is the name we use for our initial lay-pastor training time. In our small-group system, we have found that this initial training time is essential, and so we hold Super Bowls three times each year. Of course years ago we had only one Super Bowl annually, but as our small-group ministry grew and expanded, we increased the number of our Super Bowls accordingly. We now hold them on the first weekends of October, February, and May. Along with each Super Bowl, we conduct a large church-growth institute that brings people in from all over the nation. During this time we have workshops and general sessions during the day, and in the evenings, those attending the church-growth institute observe the new recruits' training in the Super Bowl.

Let me take you step by step through a Super Bowl. We begin on Thursday night with a big rally. At that time, I cast the vision of lay-driven, small-group ministry. We also have some testimonies from lay pastors. Then after about one hour and twenty minutes, the trainees move out into their districts, each of which is led by a district pastor from our staff. The pastor begins leading the recruits through the Small Group Seminar training manual, page by page. They dismiss the session at about 9:30 P.M.

We begin again on Friday night when I teach about evangelism—how to lead someone to Christ and how to follow up—and then the trainees go back to their district meetings to continue on through the training manual. During these meetings, they also spend time praying together and planning strategies for creating new groups.

On Saturday morning, we come together at 8:30 A.M. for a continental breakfast, and then I speak again at the general session—usually on prayer and the Holy Spirit. Then once again the trainees return to their district meetings. Their time will now include working through the twenty-one principles given in chapter 4 of this book, as well as in learning how to make phone calls and how to deal with EGRs. Finally they begin to plan the groups they will put together in the coming days.

After a lunch break, the trainees take an open-book test on what they've learned in the training manual. Of course we're not out to flunk anyone, but we do want to be sure they understand what is required of them and what is involved in lay-pastor ministry before they begin. About 2:00 P.M. we have a commitment service, where the trainees come forward with their commitment sheets. Following the commitment service, each trainee is scheduled for an appointment with their district pastor to go over and plan where they're going to work, in what group, and whether they're going to be an assistant or lead a new group and to clear up any questions they may still have.

One of the terms our recruits learn is *on-line.* This is a very important term that grew out of our Super Bowls. Years ago we would have many trained people coming out of the Super Bowls with no groups to go to. Then someone came up with the idea of putting up a clothesline with sheets of 8 1/2" x 11" paper hanging from it. On these sheets we wrote down each existing group as well as those we were planning to create. For each we would list the leader, the assistant leader, the host/hostess, the place, and the time.

We would begin the Super Bowl with enough sheets to meet the goals set by each district pastor. For example, if a district pastor has forty existing groups, but his or her goal is to have fifty-five groups, we put up fifty-five sheets, fifteen of which might be blank. We would do this for each district. As we go through the Super Bowl, we work with trainees to fill up those blank sheets with all the information necessary to begin new groups. Typically by the time our trainees graduate from the Super Bowl, all the sheets are full. We then say that all our groups are planned and "on-line."

What on-line does is take advantage of the enthusiasm and excitement at these Super Bowls to get the new groups going—and it works! In the following weeks, these new groups are established as our new trainees take their place in lay ministry. We have found Super Bowls and on-line to be very effective ways to work together to see our small-group ministry grow and accomplish all that we believe God has called it to.

Dealing with Volunteer Burnout

One of the things you want to watch out for in volunteers is burnout. In our experience, we're learning that no matter how good a job you may do or how well you train lay pastors, the everyday wear and tear of life can produce burnout in any of us. We expect that 20–25 percent of our lay pastors will drop out every year. Even though it's hard to lose someone in whom you've invested a lot of time and training, expecting it to happen keeps us from getting too upset when it does happen. But we believe it's important to forget our own feelings at a time like that and just concentrate on the fact that God calls us to come alongside and minister to burned-out lay leaders. That's how we find out what's going on in their lives and how we minister the love of Jesus to them. And that's how we help "recycle" them.

Let me illustrate. We had a couple who was extremely successful for many years in our lay-pastor ministry. They worked particularly with our youth, assisting our youth pastor in small groups. Then all of a sudden they stopped coming to church. When I asked the district pastor about this couple, he said, "Well, they both work full-time jobs, they have foster kids, they just bought a business, and they're really stressed out." So I told him to give them my love and concern.

Well, a few more weeks went by and I still hadn't seen them at church. One Sunday morning after preaching two services, I went home exhausted, hoping to rest while my wife fixed dinner. Pretty soon she came into the bedroom where I was lying down.

"Dale," she said, "I think you should call this couple. Here's their phone number."

I've learned over the years to listen to my wife, so I got up and made the call.

"Pastor Galloway?" said the surprised voice on the other end of the line.

"Yes," I answered. "I've been missing you at church. I know you've been very busy with your business and jobs and foster kids. But I just thought I would call and see how you are doing."

As he began to explain to me how stressed and overloaded he and his wife felt, I realized how desperately they needed a break.

"You have both been so faithful in lay-pastor ministry all these years," I said. "And I really appreciate it. But I believe it's time you and your wife took a rest for a while."

"Can we do that?" he asked.

"Of course," I said. "All I want you to do is to come and sit down front and listen to the sermon and the music and get restored."

He sounded so relieved! "Pastor," he said, "we were seriously considering leaving the church because we just couldn't bring ourselves to tell you that we weren't going to be lay pastors anymore."

The next Sunday there they were, right in the front row. In fact, every Sunday for the next several months they sat there soaking in the service and receiving healing and restoration. By the end of six months, they were right back into ministry again. They had been "recycled."

That's why it is so important not to center on our own feelings when people drop out of ministry, but rather make it a priority to come alongside and minister to them right where they are. If we assist them in their time of need and love them and work with them, then it will just be a matter of time until they're involved in ministry again. We find that whenever we handle a situation in this way, these formerly burned-out lay leaders are back at the next Super Bowl ready to be involved in lay ministry once again. Remember, it is not only our responsibility to train leaders, but to minister to and maintain those leaders. When we do, the dividends will be worth every bit of our investment.

Implementing the Vision

Do you remember the story in chapter 1, where the first person in line to go up and receive communion was actually headed for the restroom? Consequently, three or four rows of people stacked up against the restroom door before they finally figured out their leader had led them in a different direction. Again I ask you, is leadership important?

Let me answer that question this way: You show me a church that's doing well and I'll show you a church that has a strong leader—a man or woman of God—who's giving great leadership to that church. Behind every successful organization or enterprise is a leader who knows who he or she is and what to do at the right time. Strong leadership is essential to all church growth, and that's why leadership development must be a priority in every church. Although I have seen several monuments built to great leaders, I have never seen a monument built to a committee, have you?

Task Leaders and Cohesive Leaders

I believe there are two basic types of leaders, task leaders and cohesive leaders. A task leader is someone like General Patton who sees the goal and is going to get there no matter what. A cohesive leader, on the other hand, is a lover of people, someone who really enjoys connecting people together in love. I have one pastor on my staff—Jerry Smith—who is such a strong, cohesive leader, he won't even walk across the street unless everyone is holding hands.

I confess that I lean more toward being a task leader. But years ago I took the phrase in 1 Corinthians 14:1, "Follow the way of love," and I've been working hard all these years at balancing my life to become more of a cohesive leader, as well as a task leader.

Which are you? If you're a task leader, maybe you need to work a little bit more on following the way of love, of being more cohesive; if you're a cohesive leader, maybe you need to work on being more aggressive in your pursuit of the vision God has given you.

What kind of leader does a church need? It needs both. My dad was a church administrator in Ohio for more than thirty years, overseeing 140 churches in that area. I'll never forget one church in the northern part of the state. For a while, they changed pastors about every two years. Now this church had a strong lay leader who was a task leader. He also happened to be the Sunday school superintendent. He was always rising up and casting the vision for Sunday school, proclaiming, "We're going for it!" But the successive pastors—also task leaders—saw the vision differently. When they tried to butt heads with the lay leader, they discovered that he was stronger than they were. So guess who ended up leaving?

Finally my dad selected the most cohesive, loving pastor he could find to send to this church. This man just loved people. When he went to the church, almost immediately he and the lay leader hit it off. The lay leader simply couldn't resist this pastor's loving nature. They soon became friends and partners together in ministry, like two strong workhorses, teamed up and pulling in the same direction. Before long they had led that church to great accomplishment in the Lord, and they served together in harmony for many, many years.

As leaders in the church, we need to understand our own leadership style and the leadership styles of the rest of the leaders in our churches. Who are the task leaders in the church? Identify them. Who are the cohesive leaders? Identify them. As we build pastoral staffs, we need both cohesive leaders and task leaders so that we can work together and become a balanced team.

Influencing the Influencers

Who has influence in your church who will help you sell your vision? You can't take a church from where it is right now to where you believe God wants it to go unless you understand who has the influence in that church. Leadership is influence, not titles. You may find some little old lady who is not even on the board, but who has been at that church for fifty years, and everybody goes to her for prayer. She may very well be one of the strongest leaders in the church because she has influence with so many people.

So what do you do? You go over to Grandma Jones's house and ask her to pray with you. Share your heart with her, and pretty soon she'll be influencing other people for the cause you believe the church ought to pursue. But first you have to understand who has influence and then spend time influencing the influencers who, in turn, influence other people for you.

It may surprise you, but—even though I'm the founding pastor—I never take a vote in a board meeting unless I know that there's a strong consensus on that board for a particular cause, idea, or project. I work behind the scenes influencing the influencers and bringing consensus together before pursuing a board vote.

Characteristics of Great Leaders

Having studied leaders for a good part of my life—leaders in government, leaders in the military, and leaders in the church—I have discovered five basic characteristics that I see in every great leader.

1. *Leaders dream impossible dreams that change the world.*

2. *Leaders have a "can-do" spirit.* They believe that somehow, someway, this dream can become reality.

I remember the story of a man who was going to take a trip to Italy. He went to see his barber and told him about his upcoming trip. The man was really excited as he related which airline he would be flying on, which hotel he would be staying at, and the fact that, in addition to conducting some important business there, he intended to see the Pope.

Well, his negative barber started shooting down all the man's plans. He said, "That's a terrible airline you've picked. I heard one of their planes crashed last year. And that hotel! You'll hate that. No one should stay there; they have terrible service. And everyone knows you can't get any business done in Italy, so forget even trying. And as for seeing the Pope—impossible! You'll never even get near him!"

Well, the man ignored his barber and went ahead with his trip. When he returned from Italy, he went to the barber to tell him all about the wonderful time he'd had. "It was the smoothest flight I've ever experienced," he said. "And the service at the hotel was impeccable! I completed all the business I had hoped to do. And best of all, I not only saw the Pope, he actually came up and spoke to me!"

The barber was stunned. "The Pope actually spoke to you?" he asked, incredulous. "What did he say?"

"He asked me where I got such a lousy haircut," the man replied.

Negative people. They're everywhere. If you want to be a strong and effective leader, you cannot allow negative people to affect you. As a leader, it's up to you to set the sail, to keep your eyes on the vision, and to hang on to the dream. But you can only do that if you maintain a "can-do" attitude, a spirit of faith in Jesus Christ that he has called you and he's going to bring you through to victory.

3. *Leaders make it happen.* They find a way to do what God has called them to do. They know that if it doesn't happen this year, it will happen next year, or the next. If they can't get it done now, they'll come back and do it later. But somehow, someway, they will see their dream become reality. Why? Because when God created leaders, he gave them the capacity to make things happen.

According to Nicholas Murray Butler, former president of Columbia University, there are three kinds of people in the world: "Those who don't know what's happening. Those who watch what is happening. Those who make things happen."

Be a leader who makes things happen in small-group ministry in your church. There is a way!

4. *Leaders understand people and know how to motivate them and lead them to success.* Become a student of people. I once wrote a book called *64 Principles on How to Get Along with Others.* The story about one woman I remember well is a good example of applying one of those sixty-four principles.

She was a member of a church I had been called to pastor, and I had barely been there a few weeks when she began calling me. She would call me daily and go on and on and on for a couple of hours at a time. She was definitely an Extra Grace Required person! She was draining me emotionally, and I was beginning to understand why the former pastor left town. Finally I thought, "Wait a minute. I've got to set some limits here." So the next time she called I said to her, "I'll tell you what, you can call me every Friday, and I'll talk to you for fifteen minutes, but that's it. I have a lot of other people to pastor and you're draining me emotionally. I have no time or energy left for anyone else." I held her to that fifteen-minute call on Fridays. I had to set limits so that I would be free to pastor the rest of the people in the church.

Sooner or later every small-group leader runs into someone like the woman described above. It is essential that leaders understand and implement the principles of working with people that we teach in our training sessions.

5. *Leaders are successful first in managing their own lives.* Before we can manage others, we must first manage ourselves. If our own lives are out of control, how can we expect to teach others to control theirs?

Casting a Vision as a Leader

The primary job of a senior pastor is to cast the vision for the entire church. The primary task of the leader in a meta-church is to continue casting that vision. People will only rise to the occasion and volunteer when they catch the vision. Most people want to do something greater with their lives than just living for themselves. They want to make their lives count for something. It is up to us as leaders to impart a vision to them and then show them how they can be a part of fulfilling that vision.

Proverbs 29:18 says, "Where there is no vision, the people perish" (KJV). When asked about being blind, Helen Keller replied, "There's one thing worse than being blind. It's to live without vision." That is so prophetic for our churches. There is nothing worse for a church than to exist without a vision. And for a church to understand its God-given vision, it must have a leader who receives that vision through the Holy Spirit and then casts that vision for the people. Watching my father's experience as a church administrator, I remember seeing church after church without any growth. But every once in a while, some young pastor would come to these churches fresh out of Bible college. This young person may not have had any experience, but he or she had one thing: a vision, a belief that God was going to do something great through that church and through that community. And so that young leader would begin to cast the vision. "God wants to use us," the people would hear. "God wants to bring people to himself through us." And guess what would happen? Six months later, we would begin to hear that the church was experiencing some growth. But growth only occurred when someone who had caught the vision of a great God and what he wanted to do through people came to lead people who were willing to catch and pursue that vision.

Without a vision, we rarely move beyond our current boundaries. "Vision," said Jonathan Swift, "is the art of seeing things invisible." When we lose our vision, we become blind to the invisible. *Tell me your vision and dreams, and I will tell you your future.*

What is your vision for small groups in your church? Write it down. Where do you want to be six months from now, three years from now, five years from now? Write it down! How do you plan to impart this vision to your people? How do you plan to get it across to them? Remember, you will never get faithful volunteers to work as lay pastors in small-group ministry until the people catch the vision.

The very first step in conveying the vision to people is to train leaders who have already caught the vision. These leaders will build the groups, the groups will train new leaders, and those new leaders will build more groups.

Using Middle Management—Lay-Pastor Leaders

The most important job of the pastor and the pastoral staff is leadership development, training lay leaders who will build small groups. Leadership development is essential, and it must be top priority. It cannot be left to chance.

This is how lay leaders are developed at New Hope. Lay-pastor ministry begins when someone comes to the initial training time, which we call our Super Bowl. Then they serve as an apprentice in a small group for about ninety days, attending weekly training sessions throughout that time. At the end of that time, the apprentice is publicly awarded a lay-pastor badge and officially becomes a full-fledged lay pastor. After becoming a lay pastor, serving in ministry faithfully for two years, training other lay pastors, and starting new small groups, the lay pastor is eligible to become a lay-pastor leader. This is the highest level of lay-pastor ministry in our church.

We consider our lay-pastor leaders to be "middle management" at New Hope, even though they are all volunteers. Many of our pastoral staff members have come from this middle-management level, and they are now serving as district pastors.

Here is the job description for lay-pastor leaders at New Hope.

Lay-Pastor Leader Job Description

1. Perform all the ministry activities required of a lay pastor.
2. Supervise and make effective in ministry five new lay pastors.
3. Supervise five small groups and make them successful.
4. Lead a small group and continue to train new leaders from that group.

5. Look for potential leaders in small groups. Work with trainees and put them into apprentice positions in preparation for attending initial training and becoming lay pastors.
6. Keep in touch with the assigned lay pastors and keep encouraging them.

How does someone become a lay-pastor leader?

They earn it. We don't give this position away. It must be earned. We made some mistakes in the early days by giving this title to people who hadn't really earned it. We now know that we need lay-pastor leaders who are producers and reproducers of small groups and other lay pastors. It is easy to recognize these people. They are the "cream," and cream always rises to the top. These people earn their position by how they relate to their district pastor in partnership, how they carry out their ministry, and how they help fulfill the vision and dreams of their senior pastor.

They are selected. The district pastor must see in lay-pastor leaders both the fruits of and potential for their ministry. This is a judgment call by the district pastor.

They are approved. Lay-pastor leaders must be approved by the senior pastor and the other district pastors—in other words, the entire pastoral staff.

They sign a contract. Our lay pastors sign a commitment form at a Super Bowl and serve until, for whatever reason, they are no longer able to serve. Lay-pastor leaders, however, sign a written contract committing themselves to do what was described earlier in this chapter. This contract is for a one-year period. The reason we require these contracts is because lay-pastor leadership is a heavy commitment.

Every fall we have a lay-pastor leader gathering or retreat. All the lay and staff pastors are there, and we share with the lay-pastor leaders what is expected of them. The lay-pastor leaders then meet with their district pastors and begin planning their area of ministry for the coming year. It's a wonderful time of partnering together. If the terms of the contract are not carried out, the lay-pastor leader will no longer be a lay-pastor leader.

They must be productive. Lay-pastor leaders must be producers, training lay pastors and starting small groups. They are constantly recruiting, motivating, and training.

For churches that are too small to afford much staff, using lay-pastor leaders is a great way to accomplish the never-ending ministry that needs to be done.

Raising Up Lay-Pastor Leaders—A Plan

If I were just starting out in ministry today, I would start the first small group myself. I would then develop a strategy so that within two years, I would have ten groups. I would head those ten groups with leaders I had trained out of the first group. And while I was training those first leaders, I'd be watching for the ones who could become lay-pastor leaders. So after the first two years, out of all lay pastors I trained, at least two lay pastors rose to the top who were then trained to assist me with supervising those groups.

These groups can be started and leaders trained without hiring any staff at all. That is the exact reason we can do so much ministry here at New Hope. It doesn't cost any money to have lay pastors and lay-pastor leaders. And there are people in every church who would love to be involved in this kind of high-level lay ministry, partnering with the pastor to serve people.

◆8

Launching and Multiplying

If you want a successful small-group system in your
church and you want to see that small-group system
explode into church growth, you must first understand
some key factors in the process. It's important to get each
new small group off to a positive start. Starting small is the
best way to do this—ideally with one small group in the
pastor's home. Out of that group the pastor can train new
leaders for new groups. But what are the next steps that
need to be taken once those new leaders are ready to go
out and start new groups?

This is how we start new groups at New Hope. First, a
new lay leader completes a plan sheet with his or her district pastor. Then the leader schedules an appointment with
his or her district pastor to get the new group on-line, with
leaders, starting date, and location confirmed.

TLC Plan Sheet

District   Group #

Plans for Forming and Building Your TLC Group

1. Group leader
2. Assistant group leader
3. Host/hostess
4. Place where your TLC will meet
5. The date on which you're going to start
6. The regular time your meeting is going to be held
7. Build your prospect list.
8. Pray your prospect list.
9. Work your prospect list.
10. Commit yourself to attending the training session every week where your pastor will teach you and help you develop and where you will be accountable to your pastor with written reports and assignments.

To find members for the new group, we begin building a prospect list with the names, addresses, and phone numbers of people already contacted by the leadership team (leader, assistant leader, and host/hostess). This list will be the best source for future prospects. More prospects will be added from "Friendship and Communication" cards turned in to the church as well as from a computer print-out of people on our church mailing list. The leadership team can add names of neighbors, coworkers, relatives, and friends outside the church. Once the list is built, the team begins to pray the prospect list, then to work it—making phone calls and home visitations. This responsibility can be shared with others in the small group but will ultimately be successful only if the leader is leading by example.

We've had great success using a social event to kick off new small groups. We suggest that the first meeting—at the same time and location as the ongoing meetings—be a social time for people to get acquainted, fellowship over a meal or dessert, and hear the leader give a brief description of the purpose of the group. This is also an excellent time for the leader and others to share what small-group experience has meant to them. After this first social meeting, the leaders can call and personally invite each person back for the second meeting. Some people just need more than one personal invitation to get involved.

In our Small Group Seminar training manual, which is available for purchase (see p. 159), there are several helpful pages of instructions and suggestions for starting a new small group. If you order one of these manuals, please feel free to make copies of anything that will be useful to you, and adapt our instructions to fit your own needs. Why reinvent the wheel if you can use ours, right? In fact, you may want to try using the three introductory lessons provided in the manual. These are very helpful in establishing loving, trusting relationships within the group.

Assistant or Apprentice Leaders

Another key to successful small-group ministry is the leader's assistant. It is extremely important that each group have an apprentice. These apprentices are an absolute must for successful small-group ministry. I tell our leaders, "Don't wait until the Super Bowl to start training a new person. Begin training them right in the group by making them the assistant or apprentice leader. Then when the next Super Bowl comes around, bring them in to begin their official training." The apprentice is trained right in the group to launch out and start a new group. Much of our own church growth has come through the new groups that were created when apprentices became leaders.

Motivating People in Small Groups

Small groups need leaders who positively motivate people. Let's look at seven tips for positive motivation.

1. *The Holy Spirit is the motivator.* We preach and teach about the Holy Spirit often because we know that when people are filled with the Holy Spirit, they are motivated for ministry that begins to happen in and through their lives.

2. *Cast the vision.* Keep sharing how God has called you to do this great ministry and how God is calling the people to do something even greater, to make their lives really count for something. The second chapter of Nehemiah is a real illustration of vision-casting. We see there how a discouraged people living with broken-down walls were challenged by a leader who had the vision of a rebuilt city with rebuilt walls. This leader—Nehemiah, a picture of the Holy Spirit—began to cast this vision, and the people got up out of the shambles and ruins of their lives, rallied behind this leader, and began to get the job done. So if we want to get the job done—fulfill the vision God has given us—we must first cast the vision for the people so that they will want to be a part of it.

3. *Use love motivation, not guilt.* All of us have been in churches where people make us feel guilty if we don't do certain things. However, guilt motivation is short-lived. Love motivation is healthy and positive and motivates people for a lifetime of service to God.

4. *Dramatize the need.* This is one of the more creative ideas we've had come out of a staff meeting. We chose a Sunday when lay people from every one of our 210 ministries would carry signs about their ministries in the service. At a designated point, 210 lay people stood up holding their signs and marched up and down the aisles and all across the front of the sanctuary. It was a very effective way to visualize or dramatize the ministries for the con-

gregation. Then I stood up and said, "All these ministries are possible because you bring your tithes and offerings. Each one of these ministries needs more workers to accomplish the job. These are tremendous opportunities for you to use your spiritual gifts and time to make a difference in other people's lives."

5. *Help yourself by helping others.* I once read an interview with former President Jimmy Carter in which he talked about teaching Sunday school classes all his adult life. Even today he teaches Sunday school in Plains, Georgia. In fact, he plans his schedule so he will be home on Saturday night in time to prepare to speak to his class and teach them on Sunday morning. When the reporter asked President Carter why he did this, he replied, "I do this because I've learned that by helping others, I help myself." Of course, the Alcoholics Anonymous program was built on Bill Wilson's discovery that the best way for people to quit drinking was to help other people quit drinking. Helping yourself by helping others is a strong motivation to become involved in ministry, and it is based on the truth found in James 5:16: "Therefore confess your sins to each other and pray for each other so that you may be healed."

6. *Be on the inside.* In his book *Master Plan of Evangelism*, Robert Coleman points out how Jesus poured two-thirds of his time into his twelve disciples. That's interesting, isn't it? The larger portion of the Lord's ministry was not spent in public ministry, it was spent training those twelve men. And what a job he did! Look how they carried on after he was gone. Yes, they had a shaky time until they received the Holy Spirit, but then all the training they had came to the surface. They had been prepared by the Lord to launch the church!

7. *Be called of God.* I'm a pastor today because at fifteen years of age at a youth camp, I received a dramatic call from God to ministry. I was sitting looking into a campfire

when the Holy Spirit spoke to my heart and told me that if I didn't preach the gospel, thousands of people would be lost in eternal flames. I've never forgotten that. That call was literally burned into my heart that night, and it burns brighter today than ever before. I want to create an atmosphere where other people are called of God—youth, children, adults, and lay people. A call of God into ministry is a strong, strong motivation.

Motivating and Encouraging Leaders

When working with other people and overseeing them in ministry, we need to remember three things—the "Triple-A Treatment" I call it:

- Attention
- Appreciation
- Affirmation

A while back I had a staff member who was just out of step with everyone else. (To avoid identifying this person, I'll just use the name "Pat.") One day I went and sat down in Pat's office. Pat had been on my staff for a long time, and I said, "Pat, I just wanted to let you know that I appreciate you."

Pat seemed surprised. "You do? I didn't think you appreciated me anymore."

"I certainly do," I answered. "I'm really glad you're on this team."

I spent a little more time with Pat, offering attention, appreciation, and affirmation. By the time I left, I could tell things had been straightened out. From then on, everything was fine. Pat got along well with the rest of the staff, and there was no more friction. All of us need some "Triple-A Treatment" once in awhile—especially from the ones over us in leadership.

Each Christmas Eve we have what we call a "Glorious Christmas Eve" service. Actually we have two of them—one at 6:30 and one at 8:30 P.M.—when a total of more than six thousand people come together to celebrate. All of our choirs and the orchestra are there, celebrating the birth of Christ with beautiful music. Right in the middle of those Christmas Eve services, I stand up and introduce the "Lay Pastor of the Year" and describe to the congregation what this person has been doing in ministry. At the end of the service, we have a special candle-lighting event with the light-of-Jesus candle burning at the center of the stage. All the other lights are out, so the candle is the only light to be seen. Then I go forward with the staff pastors, light my candle from the light of Jesus, and turn and light the other pastors' candles with my own. At the same time, the lay pastors come down from the balcony and all over the auditorium to gather together in the front, and the staff pastors light their candles. Finally, the lay pastors move out into the congregation, carrying the light of Jesus and lighting the candles of every single person in the building. Before long, the darkness has been dispelled and everything becomes light. We hold our candles up and sing "Joy to the world, the Lord has come!" What a tremendous and thrilling experience it is to visibly present to the congregation what is being done in ministry each and every day of the year as our lay pastors move out into their neighborhoods and cities through their small groups, bringing light into a dark world. And what a wonderful way to give some "Triple-A Treatment" to those lay pastors who serve so faithfully all year long!

But don't limit your "Triple-A Treatment" to annual extravaganzas. Put some creative planning into your weekly training meetings. Use that time to minister to your lay leaders. Encourage them, build them up, and let them know they are all valuable players on the team. Believe me, that attitude will carry over into their small groups when they go out to take the week's lesson to their people.

Creating High Visibility for Small Groups

In order to have a successful small-group ministry, that ministry must have top-priority visibility. One of the ways we create high visibility is by having our lay leaders wear lay-pastor badges not only to the Sunday morning celebration services, but throughout the week at each church function they attend.

About twelve years ago, a man named Harry came to our church and we became good friends. Harry had always had a heart for ministry and a vision of what lay people could do if given the opportunity. That vision often got him into trouble in the little church he had attended before coming to New Hope. So when he came to our church and found out about lay-pastor ministry, he was really excited. He began training to become a lay pastor almost immediately, and soon he and his wife started a small group in their home. Before long he was leading people to Christ and training new leaders to start more small groups. It was as if Harry had discovered what he'd been looking for all his life.

Then about five years later, the doctors discovered he had a brain tumor. I'll never forget the last time we had lunch together. Harry was having a hard time remembering things—so much so that he had written my name in the palm of his hand so he wouldn't forget it. When I spoke at his funeral soon after that, I was overwhelmed with the sight of the crowd. About twelve hundred people had come to honor Harry. Although he had been a rather quiet man, he had impacted so many lives.

Before he died, Harry had made one last request of his family. He said to them, "When I'm lying in the casket, make sure they put my lay-pastor badge on me." And so as people filed by his casket by the hundreds, there on his coat was his badge, which read, "Harry Vawter, Lay Pastor, New Hope Community Church." Harry wore his badge with pride, both as he served among us and as his body lay in his casket.

This is a wonderful example of what serving in our lay ministry means to our lay pastors. It is important to them. We honor and respect and appreciate them. We give them high visibility by talking about them to others, including them in sermons, recognizing them publicly, and telling everyone in our new membership classes about the opportunities available to them as lay pastors. And of course, we pray for them constantly in pastoral prayer time.

We have found that these small investments on our part pay great dividends as our small-group ministry multiplies into explosive church growth.

9

Integrating Small Groups into Your Church

I believe that God has given us a biblical formula for implementing an effective small-group ministry in our churches. That formula is found in Acts 20:20, which reads: "You know that I have not hesitated to preach anything that would be helpful to you but have taught you publicly and from house to house"—which represents both large- and small-group ministry.

When someone has good, clear vision, we say they have 20/20 vision. Isn't it amazing that God's plan for effective ministry can be seen so clearly in Acts 20:20? Let's examine the 20/20 vision God has given us.

There are two parts to that vision, like two sides to a coin—the celebration service and the small groups. I love them both, and they are equally important to the life of our church. In fact, I believe we need both to accomplish what God has called us to do here at New Hope.

My children provide an illustration of this idea. If someone asks me, "Which one of your two children do you love the most?" how could I possibly answer them? Margi and I have a daughter named Ann, a beautiful, 5'2", blue-eyed blonde who looks a lot like her mother. Ann attends Azusa Pacific University in southern California, and we are extremely proud of her. We also have a son named Scott who is 6'5", weighs about 250 pounds, and is about to graduate from high school. Scott has a way of looking down at me and saying, "Hi, Dad," in that deep voice of his that just melts my heart. So which child do I love the most? Both of them. Which one is more important? They are both important! There is simply no other way to answer those questions.

And so it is with 20/20 vision and the church. The weekly celebration service is a glorious time when everyone from all our small groups comes together to worship God and to celebrate his goodness toward us. As the church grows, so the celebration becomes greater. Our choirs and orchestra lead us in a wonderful time of praise and worship; we have a special time of prayer and teaching of the Word; and we go home refreshed, renewed, and ready for the week that lies ahead.

And then there are the small groups—people coming together in various times and places throughout the greater-Portland metropolitan area to fellowship and care for one another and to reach out to their communities with the love of Christ. How could we ever choose which we love more or which is more important?

Throughout the Book of Acts, we see that the early church had both celebration times and small-group meetings. In fact, this two-sided coin goes all the way back to the Old Testament. Do you remember when the children of Israel went into Canaan and scattered throughout the territory? Within their own small communities, the people would gather together for sharing, caring, prayer, and encouragement. But they would also come together from all their different communities to celebrate during special festivals and feast days. Often during these large celebrations, the people would sing from the Psalms, which is something we also do today. So we can see God's 20/20 vision in operation throughout both the Old and New Testaments.

Now if this balance between large celebration services and small-group meetings was in evidence in biblical times, there must be a way to incorporate that balance into church systems today. That's what I want to discuss in detail in this final chapter because, although all churches have some form of weekly celebration or worship service, few have balanced those services with small-group ministry. If we are going to effectively carry out what God has assigned his church to do—fulfill the Great Commission of disciples making disciples as well as care for and meet the needs of the people—we must find a way to balance these two elements of healthy church life.

Choices to Consider Before Starting Small Groups

Once a church realizes their need for small-group ministry and decides it is time to move ahead in that direction, they should consider the following choices and decide how small groups should look in their church.

Open or closed groups? Closed groups are restricted and dead-end, and they do not fulfill the Great Commission. At New Hope we are committed to open groups. However, we do have one exception at this point, an eight-week session for our grief-recovery group that works well because it carries its members through the process of grief into healing. But all other groups are open and committed to evangelism and outreach. That's why they are thriving and multiplying.

Short-term or ongoing groups? Ninety-eight percent of our groups are ongoing. We don't believe in short-term groups because we would always be starting over from the beginning rather than building on what is already in place.

Who should be in the groups? Should groups include members of the sponsoring church only, people affiliated with other churches, and/or people not affiliated with any church? We want everyone who belongs to our church to be involved in our small-group system, and we work hard to see that happen. But we also want people from other churches and those who have no church background to be a part of our groups. People who are affiliated with other churches are part of the church at large, as we are. Those who have no church are the ones we want to reach and bring to Christ. There is room for all of us in the small-group system.

On-premises or off-premises meetings? At New Hope, we have on-premises as well as off-premises meetings. We have groups meeting in the church every day and every night of the week. We also have groups that meet in homes, restaurants, office buildings, and warehouses throughout the city. We never want to limit people in their meeting places.

One day or night or many different meeting times? We personally prefer to allow our group leaders to choose any time of day or night that works well for them and their group. We find that this freedom produces the best results in healthy, continued growth.

Staff-led or lay-led groups? Again, we have both. We want each member of our pastoral staff to be involved in leading groups because that is the best way for them to train leaders to start other groups. However, 95 percent of our groups are now led by trained lay people.

Teacher-led or facilitator-led groups? We choose to have facilitators rather than teachers lead our groups because we have found that we can reproduce facilitators much more easily than teachers. We look for facilitators who love people and can guide them through a lesson.

Nurture- or task-oriented groups? We have both kinds of groups in our system. Some are nurturing and some nurture and also carry out tasks.

Give people a choice or assign them to groups? I think one of the worst things you can do is assign people to small groups. We have had much better results offering any help and guidance we can to assist people in finding the group best suited to their needs and then allowing them to choose the group they will attend.

Include leader training or have no training? We have initial as well as ongoing training for all our lay leaders. Leader training is extremely important for making any small-group system successful.

Include group supervision or have no supervision? I confess that there have been times when we've been a little lax in supervising our groups, and we've had to come right back and put new strength into our groups by supervising them regularly once again. We see much better results when we do this, both in what occurs in the group and in producing new groups.

Provide lessons or leave leaders on their own? Years ago we just let leaders do whatever they wanted to in their groups. We have since found that we see much better results when we provide a lesson for them. Also, these lessons are based on what's being taught in the Sunday celebration services, so everybody is heading in the same direction. Providing lessons also keeps the leaders coming to weekly training to pick up their lesson plans.

Include children in the groups or keep them separate? Again, we allow each group to decide whether to include children, have a separate program for them, or get babysitters. We have all kinds of groups in our system.

Expect leader accountability or no accountability? I firmly believe that one of the keys to a successful small-group system is accountability. I once had a pastor ask me if I was afraid of having all these groups with lay people leading them. He wondered if the leaders might not be disloyal and cause division in the church. As I thought about his question, I realized we have never had a problem with that in all the years we've been involved in small-group ministry. I believe it's because we have such a good system of accountability in place. People who are not willing to be accountable will not make good leaders; they are potential rebels who will eventually cause problems in the church.

Goals of pastoral care or evangelism? Our groups see both pastoral care and evangelism as their objectives. Although each group may fulfill those objectives differently, both are being accomplished.

An appendage, department, or totally integrated system? If you want to see the maximum benefit of small-group ministry in your church, I strongly recommend a totally integrated system. As you're building a staff, be sure each member understands that it's their job to recruit, train, and equip lay pastors and to lead small groups in their area of ministry. If your church already has staff in place who are not in favor of a fully integrated system, you will have to begin to change things gradually. Try to encourage existing staff members to come into line with your way of thinking. But if they won't, you will have to replace them in time with those who have a vision for the fully integrated small-group system. Only when every staff member sees small-group ministry as a priority will the congregation perceive it in the same way.

Tips for Starting Small Groups in a Traditional Church

Implementing the 20/20 vision in a traditional church can be a challenge. Here are some ideas, tips, and strategies to help you make it happen.

Share your vision with key leaders who are the influencers in your church. You can do that by loaning them this book, letting them listen to my tape series, or taking them to a seminar. Enlarge their vision, take their blinders off, and help them see what the 20/20 vision can accomplish in your church!

When we were a small church just starting out, I used to take my leaders to southern California every year to a conference at a very large church. I would tell them, "Someday we are going to be a church of thousands of people," even though we were just a humble handful at the time.

Do not forget that your church has a history and traditions. It is unfair to ignore people who have been in the church for a long time—possibly much longer than the leadership who wants to make this change. You must be respectful of them. I remember one pastor who came to a church, and the first thing he did was do away with the men's ministry. Before long he had also done away with the Sunday school as well as a long-standing annual event that many in the church looked forward to each year. In fact, he did away with everything traditional and dear to the church's members. The following year, the members did away with the pastor and replaced him with one who was more sensitive to their traditions.

Take an inventory of groups, resources, and opportunities already present in your church. Make lists of your existing groups, then write down the needs within your community that could be met through need-meeting small groups. You may be surprised at the opportunities already within your reach.

Know your people. For example, people who were born before World War II are more fearful of intimacy than people born after that time. It's the way they were brought up, and you need to be respectful of that. You can work with them by suggesting they attend a small group but assuring them they don't need to participate verbally if they don't want to. Make every effort to ease people into changes. Make them comfortable by understanding and respecting their individual personalities.

Plan where you want your small-group ministry to be five years from now. Remember, what I'm sharing with you in this book didn't happen overnight, or even in a year or two. We have been building it for twenty years from the ground up, block upon block upon block. It takes planning, and it takes time.

Break down your master plan into manageable steps. How do you eat an elephant? You do it one bite at a time. So plan now where you want to go in three months, six months, and one year. It seems much less overwhelming that way.

Write down what you're going to do in the next three months to take small groups in your church to the next level. Always put in writing what you need to do to move forward—never get stuck at your present level, but keep pressing on to the next one.

Practice this wise principle: Do not threaten, but expand. I was doing a seminar on small groups in the East when a pastor came up to me. He had written on a piece of paper these words: "Do not threaten, but expand." I was really impressed with the thought, and he gave me permission to share the concept with others. I encourage you to be careful you don't threaten people with the implementation of the 20/20 vision in your church, but rather expand slowly until it is achieved. The best way to do this is to work with your existing staff (old track) to change their way of thinking while allowing the train to continue down the familiar track. At the same time, put a new track in place around the perimeter of the church—start small groups and raise up leaders for more small groups—until the new track eventually replaces the old one.

A pastor friend of mine in southern California, Larry DeWitt, recently told me that's exactly what is happening in his church. For years they operated closed or covenant groups only. The previous summer, however, Larry had caught the vision for what could be done through open groups and had committed to changing over to an open-group system. Because he already had a staff in place who believed in closed groups, he wisely allowed for a gradual change by instituting a three-year changeover plan. This plan would convert the system from closed to open and from the old track to the new track, without threatening those who were already running on the old track.

Begin with a model group or groups. We've had churches of every denomination and size come to us and ask, "How do we start?" We always tell them to start small. The rule of thumb is to have one model group for about every one hundred members. Of course that ratio is flexible, but it seems to work best when followed as closely as possible.

The pastor (or pastors) should lead the model groups, setting the pace for the rest of the congregation. Out of the model groups, the pastor trains new leaders who then go out and start new groups. The multiplication process begins immediately and continues on indefinitely. Once enough new leaders have been raised up, it is time to start an initial training time, such as our Super Bowl, and to institute ongoing training as well. This type of beginning is much more effective than announcing from the pulpit one Sunday morning that you are starting a small-group ministry in the church and then asking people to sign up. Start small, build a strong foundation, and then go from there.

Take the time to make the change gradually. You've heard the old "frog in the kettle" story, haven't you? If you want to cook a live frog, put him in a kettle of cool water, then turn up the fire underneath the kettle one degree at a time.

The frog won't even notice the difference and will stay in the water until he's "done." If you turn the heat up all at once, however, he will jump out almost immediately.

Build some flexibility into your small-group system. We have procedures, principles, and expectations for our group leaders, but we also have some flexibility to work with individual needs and personalities. One thing I've noticed about trees—they stand strong if they are flexible in the wind. If they're rigid, they break. Keep that in mind when working with people.

Love people into it. Across from my office on the I-205 freeway is the biggest shopping center in the Northwest. Last Christmas a teenaged girl took her little brother, who was mentally handicapped, shopping for last-minute gifts. The crowds were rushing around, pushing and shoving each other in their hurry to finish and go home. In the midst of it, someone pushed the little boy into a rack full of shoes. The shoes fell to the floor and the harried salesman turned on the little boy.

"Pick up those shoes!" ordered the salesman.

The little boy was frightened and confused so he said, "No."

The salesman continued to yell at the little boy, the boy continued to refuse, and a crowd gathered. Then the teenaged girl bent down and began to pick up the shoes. Soon her little brother was helping her. When they finished, the girl looked at the salesman and said, "Mister, you gotta love him into it."

We can't make people do anything. If we want to take them to another level in their life with Christ, we just gotta love 'em into it in Jesus' name.

Gradually change your staff into people who will build their ministries using small groups. Again, the key word here is *gradually.*

Give priority to prayer and to the Holy Spirit. I don't think it's an accident that the largest churches in the world are in Seoul, Korea. And it is not an accident that these churches have large cell systems. It is certainly not an accident that every one of those cell groups is driven by a strong prayer ministry. Make prayer a priority because the power and the presence of the Holy Spirit in your entire small-group system will make all the difference as you work together to accomplish God's work on this earth.

In Conclusion

I believe that a long time ago God planned for this time on earth and for the needs and problems that would be unique to this generation. There is so much isolation, fragmentation, pain, and brokenness in this world today, and nothing meets these needs better than a loving, small-group, family-type ministry.

I also believe there are people reading this book who will build greater churches and ministries than we've built here at New Hope by using some of this information as a foundation, people who will see the fulfillment of their God-given vision in the life of their church. May God bless you as you move ahead in pursuit of that vision.

Appendix A

Answers to the Eleven Most-Asked Questions about Small Groups

Question 1: I'd like to start a small-group ministry in our church, but I don't know where to begin. What do you suggest?

Answer 1: The first thing to do is spend much time in prayer to be sure this is God's plan for your church. Then if you believe it is, take inventory of the groups you already have—task groups such as ushers or office volunteers, care or discipleship groups, and support groups. Every church has people gathered in groups, so use those groups as a logical starting point.

The next thing I would advise is to start small. Our natural tendency is to divide up the entire parish and say, "Okay, these people go with this leader, these people over here with that leader," and so on because we want to see it *big* and *now.* But that's not the way to successful small-group ministry. Begin small and then add to it block by block.

Next, begin a model group. I think it's very important that the pastor or all the pastors be involved in leading that model group or groups. As a rule of thumb, you should have one model group for each one hundred church members. For instance, if you have six hundred members and three or four pastoral staff members, you should start with three to six model groups. If you have fewer than one hundred members, one model group is sufficient with the pastor leading that group. This way the pastor learns small-group ministry from the ground up and will be comfortable with the concept as it grows. Your next goal will be to train new leaders from the model group who can start other groups. You should be ready to start that second generation of groups within three to five months.

Go as far as the second generation before making a great big announcement to get people involved in small groups. And a word of caution to pastors: One of our biggest problems is that we like to talk. Remember when leading a small group to be a *facilitator*, not a teacher or preacher. Our goal is group participation, and we get that best by becoming one of the group.

Question 2: This is a great concept, but don't you think it's a little dangerous having all these lay people out there leading groups?

Answer 2: Who's it dangerous for? Whose church is it? Who's in charge? I believe the Holy Spirit is in charge, and if the church as a group becomes unhealthy, the Holy Spirit will cleanse his church. However, we have to learn to trust lay people with ministry. Of course, you have to have accountability built into your small-group system, as we do at New Hope. We have weekly report sheets that keep leaders accountable. We also have weekly training, another point of accountability. If people aren't willing to fill out reports and come to training, then they are rebellious, and rebellious people do not belong in lay ministry. We want our lay leaders to cooperate and work together as a team; there is no room for rebels. Because of this accountability system, it is amazing how small and few our problems have been through the years.

I know this question is a genuine concern for pastors, and I understand that concern. But we need to ask God to help us be more secure in our position as pastor and leader. At the same time, we need to free lay people to be involved in ministry. The only way we'll extend our ministry is by giving it away, involving lay people, letting them do it, and trusting the Holy Spirit. But it's imperative that we have a built-in accountability system with supervision that encourages and builds that team spirit.

Question 3: How large should a small group become before it's divided?

Answer 3: The ideal number for good group dynamics and for caring and dialogue is somewhere between eight and twelve. Participation is much greater when you stay within those numbers. Add more, and it's much more difficult to get people to interact and participate. It becomes very difficult for one leader to give the kind of care people need, especially between meetings, when a group grows to more than twelve people.

When groups grow large, we don't divide, we multiply. We are leader-centered. We build groups with leaders. So instead of saying, "Okay, we've got too many in this group, let's break it up," we work on recruiting new leaders in the group, bring them to initial training, and prepare and challenge them to go out and start a new group. Some of the people from the existing group will go with this new leader to help start the new group. The result is two groups with growth potential. Every time you train a new leader, you can have a new group.

We've all seen times when something dynamic is going on and the pastor or overseer goes in and tries to divide a group in two. What usually happens is you lose both groups. But by multiplying with new leaders, and giving people a choice, you end up with two growing groups.

Question 4: How do small groups affect Sunday school?

Answer 4: I have heard other small-group leaders say that to have a successful small-group system, you must do away with Sunday school entirely. I don't agree. I believe strongly in Sunday school. What we have done is break out of the Sunday-school-at-11-A.M.-only box.

Southern Baptists did a great job with Sunday school by equipping, training, and motivating new teachers. Each new teacher would then gather a group of ten people around him or her, and the church would grow through the Sunday school program. We operate on the same principle here at New Hope, but not just through the Sunday school program. We do it every day of the week with all kinds of ministry groups in all kinds of places and ways and by training facilitators rather than teachers.

We have a children's ministry that takes place in classes on Sunday morning, but we also have Kids' Clubs throughout the week in different neighborhoods as well as great evangelism outreaches. And we have similar ministries for junior and senior high students. At the adult level on Sunday we have Bible classes, a remarried class, a young marrieds class, and a seniors class. These groups are larger than our small groups but a few have only ten to fifteen people. As you can see, our Sunday school is intermixed and interrelates with everything we do in small-group ministry.

Question 5: When small groups meet in people's homes, what do you do with the children who come with their parents?

Answer 5: Because we're leader-centered, it is up to each small group's leadership to decide what to do with children.

They have many different options.

- We have children who have their own small group that meets separately in another room or house next door, with a lay pastor leading them through the same three things the adults do: share life, pray for each other, and study a Bible lesson. Children look forward to their group as much as the adults do.
- The adults get babysitters. I believe that some of the best money you can ever spend is when you hire capable childcare workers to care for small children so as many people as possible can participate in support/recovery groups.
- Some of our children meet with the adults and then, about halfway through, go into another part of the house.
- Some of the children all go to one of the adult's homes and then all the adults go to a different home for their group meeting.
- In some groups the children actually participate throughout. I was in some of those groups myself in the early days and saw that it was really meaningful for those children. We have found that children are on their best behavior in that setting.
- We have all kinds of support groups that meet every day of the week. In so many of those support groups, the children have great needs. For example, the child of an alcoholic who has been brought up in a dysfunctional family has special needs. So we have Posi-

tive Affirmation groups just for these children. Trained, professional workers lead these groups, and we've seen some great results. In fact, these leaders have written their own literature, which you can obtain by calling our church and requesting it.

Question 6: Where do you find leaders for these small groups, and how do you train them?

Answer 6: We get them from people who come to know the Lord in the small groups. New Christians are enthusiastic. They may not know much and more than likely haven't attended any sort of Bible school, so we don't throw them into a major leadership position immediately. We start them off as a host or hostess, working with them right where they are with on-the-job training before they become stagnant or lose their enthusiasm.

Training is very important. We have initial training time, which is a whole weekend. We also have ongoing training every week. So lay pastors receive training all the time on ministry and the Christian life. They also receive prepared lessons for each week. Using this method, new Christians grow up in ministry, and it becomes a way of life for them.

We have developed an entire leadership training kit— six hours of tapes and a workbook—which is available from our church upon request and can be used to implement leader training in any church.

Question 7: How do you implement this small-group ministry in a traditional church that doesn't currently have small groups?

Answer 7: I once pastored a very old, traditional church that was set in its ways. Someone once said that the seven last words of the church are, "We've never done it that way before." Well, I experienced the reality of that quickly at this church.

This church hadn't had any new people for years, and that didn't bother them in the least. So to stay alive spiritually, I started reading a number of books, many of them about small-group ministry. Then I went downtown and got acquainted with about five or six businessmen who didn't attend any church. I rented a private room at a hotel and invited the businessmen to come to a Bible study. To my surprise, they came. We met every Wednesday morning and went through the Gospel of John, verse by verse, asking these questions: What does it say? What does it mean? How do you use it in your life? We even had a little prayer time. Well, at the end of six weeks, four of those men gave their hearts to Jesus Christ. That was the most exciting thing I'd seen happen since coming to that church.

Then I found some women in the church who I believed had a heart for evangelism and challenged them to start neighborhood groups. They accepted my challenge, and pretty soon they had new people coming into those groups.

What had happened was we had instituted small groups and attracted new people around the edges of the traditional church without disturbing the church's existing traditions. Eventually the new people in the small groups began to come to the church, bringing a fresh new life with them. It was wonderful!

And that's how you institute small groups into the traditional church—slowly and carefully, without disturbing or threatening the existing structure. Eventually the new life will replace the deadness, and the church will regain its health.

Question 8: Should we have closed groups or open groups?

Answer 8: For many years in this country, small-group ministry was strictly closed or covenant groups. People met for a set period of time to do a set activity, like a study.

No one brought new people to the group, and when the activity was done, so was the group.

At New Hope, we do not have closed groups. We firmly believe in open groups that exist indefinitely and are always willing to accept new members. Even in the summer, we still have almost four thousand people each week in small groups. By continuing the groups year-round, we don't have to start all over every fall. The groups are already in place.

One of the greatest things that happens in open small groups is evangelism. Small groups are an outreach in their neighborhoods, but if the groups are closed and cannot bring in new people, they are closed to evangelizing. Small groups, just like the church itself, need new people to keep them fresh and alive. We cannot afford to allow them to become stagnant.

Question 9: These are obviously tremendous success principles for ministry. How do you go about starting a new small group?

Answer 9: Take a look at our "TLC Plan Sheet" on p. 122. On that sheet are spaces for the group leader, assistant leader, host/hostess, place of meeting, starting date, regular meeting time, prospect list, and instructions to pray and work the prospect list. To start a new group, our district pastors and group leaders go over this plan sheet in detail and begin to build a list of names, addresses, and phone numbers of prospective group members. This list is usually a combination of relatives, neighbors, and coworkers of the group leaders as well as people within the church. The pastor urges the leaders to pray over this list and then to go out and begin to invite these people to the group.

Once the people have been invited, we usually have some sort of informal social event for the first meeting—maybe a potluck meal or coffee and dessert—so people can get to know each other and become comfortable in the group. Then the leaders explain what to expect in group meetings and invite people back the next week for the first official meeting.

The key words here are: *build, pray,* and *work* the prospect list. Successful new groups are born this way.

Question 10: What is the purpose of small groups?
Answer 10: We have four purposes for our small groups:

- *Evangelism*—We want to reach the unchurched for Jesus.
- *Discipling*—Eighty percent of our new members have never belonged to a church before. So we have an enormous task of discipling. But we couldn't begin to disciple these people if we didn't have the great small-group ministry and network that we have.
- *Shepherding*—Our pastoral care occurs in these small groups. No one pastor can take care of all the people. No staff can, either. The people are cared for through small-group ministry.
- *Service*—I know of no place in the church that provides a greater opportunity for lay people to use their spiritual gifts and to be involved in meaningful service than in small groups.

Question 11: Where do you find your weekly lessons?
Answer 11: You can find lessons in many places—every Christian bookstore and denomination has lessons for small groups. But there are several qualities you should look for to find effective lessons.

- We believe that lessons should be life-centered, with practical application and truth. Our goal is Bible application, not just Bible knowledge.

- Good lessons ask good questions, the kind that cannot be answered with just yes or no. We're after dialogue and interaction.
- Some of the questions need to be non-threatening, the kind every person can answer whether he or she knows the Bible or not. We're looking for participation, and on these questions, people who don't have a great deal of Bible knowledge will be able to interact and share too.
- Some of the questions need to be the kind that can only be answered by looking up a verse. This is vital because the Bible is our authority, our Word from the Lord.
- Some of the questions need to be personal, probing into what a person has experienced and what he or she is thinking. As people share out of their experience, they learn from one another. For example, in stewardship lessons we had this year, some of the greatest teaching occurred when people shared their own experience of giving. People who are struggling with that particular area in their lives really listen to others in the group.
- The lesson should include questions that invite more than one answer, and maybe can even raise other questions for the group. These questions raise the interest level and draw people into the discussion.
- Remember that no matter how carefully you prepare the lesson, it will only be a facilitator for meeting the needs of the people. We tell our leaders that if someone expresses a need in the middle of the lesson, don't wait until the end of the lesson to respond to that need. Stop right there and respond to and pray for that need.

Our support groups at New Hope use the Twelve Steps and other material appropriate to their particular needs, such as walking through grief or divorce recovery, so their lessons are all different. But all other group leaders receive the same lesson in training each week, a lesson I've written that ties into the Sunday morning service.

I used to think that when I preached a sermon people understood it, went out, and used it. Now I realize that it takes a long time for people to understand and appropriate something into their lives. I believe the application level of the sermon goes way up when it is discussed in small groups during the week following the sermon. In fact, I believe we are discipling people in the Lord much more quickly and effectively because of this system. It keeps everyone going in the same direction and is a wonderful opportunity to put a particular emphasis into the church.

Elements of a Healthy Small Group

For visualization purposes, we're going to refer to a small group as a "cell." If you look at the diagram of a healthy cell, you will notice that we have represented that cell group by a large circle. At the top of that circle an X represents the leader or facilitator of that cell group. Every cell needs a leader. To the right of the leader, an L represents the overseer/observer of the group—in our case, a district pastor or a lay-pastor leader.

Continuing clockwise, the S represents seekers. Every healthy cell should include seekers, people who don't yet know Christ but who are searching for answers. Seekers are usually present in a cell because someone in the group who already knows Christ has brought them.

The empty chair is an important component of the healthy cell. This chair reminds us that there is someone else who needs to be a part of the group, and it is up to the group's members to bring that person in. Always keep an

Figure 7

A Healthy Cell

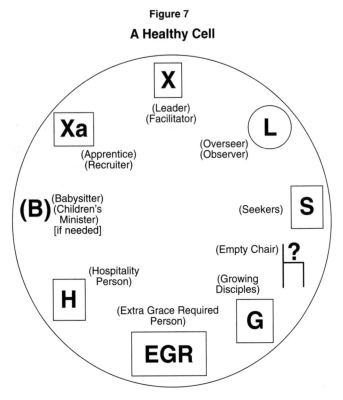

From *Prepare Your Church for the Future* by Carl F. George, Revell, 1991. Used with permission.

empty chair in the group to prevent complacency on the part of the group's members.

The G represents growth, not just in numbers but in individual growth. Remember, the Great Commission calls us to make disciples, not just converts, and disciples never stop growing.

Every cell will have its share of EGRs, those Extra Grace Required people who will challenge the group at the point of growth, both numerically as well as individually. As I mentioned before, EGRs must be dealt with firmly, quickly, and lovingly. If the situation can be dealt with within the group in such a way that the EGR person adapts to the group and no longer drains life from it, that's wonderful. If not, it is up to the cell's leadership to do whatever is necessary to assist that EGR person to find the help he or she needs elsewhere, so that the group can continue on in a healthy fashion.

The hospitality person, represented by the letter H, is an extremely important part of a healthy cell. Occasionally we have training times for our hosts and hostesses, to help them learn ways to make people feel comfortable and welcome in their home.

Moving to the letter B, which is the babysitter and/or children's minister, we see another vital element of a healthy cell group. Whether the group elects to include children in the entire meeting time, to leave them with a babysitter, to provide a lesson for them during the group discussion time, or any of a variety of options, this decision must be made by the group's leadership based on the needs of the group members.

Now we come to that key person in any healthy cell group, shown here as Xa, the apprentice to the group leader. No cell can be healthy and reproduce itself without an apprentice leader in place who assists the leader and is preparing to start a new group when the time comes for cell multiplication. And with all of these components in place, that multiplication time will definitely come!

To request materials discussed in this book,
please contact:

New Hope Community Church
1-800-935-4673